"Patrick Henry breaks open the essence of Benedictinism to the modern world. He provides the elements of a world imbedded in the basics of life when the rest of the world tilts toward its extremes. He gives us vectors to steer by—community, tradition, hospitality, productivity, and stewardship, as well as an immersion in the spiritual heart of life. He presents Benedictinism as a mirror to the world around it as it defines and redefines itself from age to age."

—Joan Chittister, OSB

"At a time when so many societies are damaged by divisive ideology, naked greed, and lust for power, this book helps us to see there is another way. In these pages we find monastics—ordinary people living an extraordinary life of prayer and community—who make us realize that grounding oneself in love and hospitality is not ancient, but always new, and more relevant than ever."

—Kathleen Norris, author of *The Cloister Walk* and
Acedia & Me: A Marriage, Monks, and a Writer's Life

"From a person deeply engaged in Benedictine communities comes this learned reflection on the charism of this Christian tradition. Patrick Henry has aptly described the 'rootedness and far-ranging adventure' of the Benedictines. Rather than withdrawing from the world, these vowed Christians engage it with humor, stability, interfaith curiosity, and their life of prayer, a pathway of generative living. Readers will be drawn to this vision of expressed faith, especially since the wisdom of the Benedictines is not relegated solely to cloistered life. It is for the world, truly."

—Molly T. Marshall, PhD, Interim President
United Theological Seminary of the Twin Cities

"Patrick Henry's new book expands the growing literature on living the Rule of St. Benedict for ordinary people. He points out many options in the Rule that could apply to anyone: listening, hospitality, discipline, persistence, and reminds us that for Benedict the monastery was a lay community. Laypeople wanting to deepen their faith and Christian living will find much valuable guidance in this well-written book."

—William O. Paulsell, author of *Longing for God: An Introduction to Christian Mysticism*

"Here is a vigorous, optimistic exposition of the contemporary Benedictine charism. This is a book for which we should all be grateful. It makes for energizing and encouraging reading. Written equally for monastic and non-monastic, we are given a survey which shows the development and expansion of Benedictine options in today's world."

—Esther de Waal, author of *The Way of Simplicity*

"I am so grateful to Patrick Henry for writing this book as a reflection on and response to Rod Dreher's *The Benedict Option*. Henry reads Dreher's work with a deserved critical eye and ear, helping the reader to take the questions that concern Dreher seriously. However, he simultaneously challenges the monochromatic view of the 'Benedict option' that Dreher insists on and shares his experiences of the many different ways to live a faithful Christian life following the Rule of Benedict. Henry's is a generous, capacious view of human faithfulness to the Gospel in the midst of the real and actual world we find ourselves in."

—Abbot John Klassen, OSB

Benedictine Options

*Learning to Live
from the Sons and Daughters
of Saints Benedict and Scholastica*

Patrick Henry

LITURGICAL PRESS
Collegeville, Minnesota

www.litpress.org

Cover design by Ann Blattner. *To the Ends of the Earth*, Donald Jackson with contributions from Sally Mae Joseph and Andrew Jamieson, © 2002 *The Saint John's Bible*, Saint John's University. All rights reserved. Scripture quotations are from the New Revised Standard Version of the Bible, Catholic Edition, © 1993, 1989 National Council of the Churches of Christ in the United States of America. Used by permission. All rights reserved.

Scripture quotations are from New Revised Standard Version Bible © 1989 National Council of the Churches of Christ in the United States of America. Used by permission. All rights reserved worldwide.

2	3	4	5	6	7	8	9

Library of Congress Cataloging-in-Publication Data

Names: Henry, Patrick, 1939– author.
Title: Benedictine options : learning to live from the sons and daughters of Saints Benedict and Scholastica / Patrick Henry.
Description: Collegeville, Minnesota : Liturgical Press, [2021] | Includes bibliographical references. | Summary: "An examination of the Benedictine way of life that demonstrates its range of options as accessible to anyone, whether lay or religious" — Provided by publisher.
Identifiers: LCCN 2021015225 (print) | LCCN 2021015226 (ebook) | ISBN 9780814666814 (paperback) | ISBN 9780814666852 (epub) | ISBN 9780814666852 (mobi) | ISBN 9780814666852 (pdf)
Subjects: LCSH: Benedictines—Spiritual life. | Monastic and religious life. | Benedictines—Rules. | Benedict, Saint, Abbot of Monte Cassino. Regula. | Benedict, Saint, Abbot of Monte Cassino. | Scholastica, Saint, active 6th century.
Classification: LCC BX3003 .H46 2021 (print) | LCC BX3003 (ebook) | DDC 255/.106—dc23
LC record available at https://lccn.loc.gov/2021015225
LC ebook record available at https://lccn.loc.gov/2021015226

To

Dolores Schuh, CHM
Wilfred Theisen, OSB

Valued colleagues at the Collegeville Institute
for Ecumenical and Cultural Research
and dear friends

and in memory of

Dietrich Reinhart, OSB
Shaun O'Meara, OSB

Contents

Acknowledgments

I am grateful to the American Benedictine Academy for invitations to speak to their conventions in 1990 and 2004; to the Benedictine Novice Institute for a similar invitation in 1991; to the American Cassinese Congregation Forty-Eighth General Chapter in 2004; and to the Saint Benedict's Monastery Council in 2006.

The World Council of Churches provided incentive to formulate my ideas about monasticism and ecumenism for a Faith and Order consultation in Singapore in 1986.

Monastic Interreligious Dialogue honored me with an invitation to moderate a conversation between Buddhist and Christian monastics at the 1993 Parliament of the World's Religions in Chicago; to serve as interface between participants and observers at the Gethsemani Encounter in 1996; and to edit a book that emerged from that event, *Benedict's Dharma: Buddhists Reflect on the Rule of Saint Benedict*.

Studium, the research center at Saint Benedict's Monastery, where I have been a day scholar since 2004, has provided countless occasions for illuminating conversations with Benedictines who have carried on the tradition of "good trouble" that began when a monk bemoaned, "Now the sisters are coming" (see p. 63).

Valuable advice, both general and specific, has been given by Nancy Bauer, OSB; Ann Marie Biermaier, OSB; Kristin Colberg; Delores Dufner, OSB; Theodore Gill; Lewis Grobe, OSB; Ephrem

Hollerman, OSB; William Skudlarek, OSB; and Columba Stewart, OSB.

The librarians at the College of Saint Benedict and Saint John's University were very helpful sleuths, as I'm sure they and their colleagues throughout the country and world have been for many others as well, when the coronavirus pandemic foreclosed physical access to their holdings. Similar thanks go to David Klingeman, OSB, Saint John's Abbey archivist, who retrieved the 1857 letter that laments the arrival of the sisters; Mariterese Woida, OSB, Saint Benedict's Monastery archivist, who retrieved the funeral homily for Jeremy Hall, OSB; and Tim Ternes, director of *The Saint John's Bible*, for help in fashioning the note on the cover.

The folks at Liturgical Press are a delight to work with: Peter Dwyer, Hans Christoffersen, Brian Woods, Ann Blattner, Tara Durheim, Stephanie Lancour, Deb Eisenschenk, Angela Steffens, Colleen Stiller, and Michelle Verkuilen.

The influence of my wife, Pat Welter, alumna of the College of Saint Benedict, is pervasive in this book. She has been close to Benedictines for almost her whole life, beginning in eighth grade. In 2009 she received from Saint Benedict's Monastery the *Mother Benedicta Riepp Award*, named after the monastery's foundress (1825–62), which recognizes a laywoman who exemplifies Benedictine and gospel values in her daily life. In her career as public schoolteacher and principal, and in her engagement with work for racial, social, gender, ecclesiastical, and economic justice, Pat has woven together numerous skeins of Benedictine options.

part one

Option or Options

Is it preposterous to prescribe Saint Benedict as the antidote to our cultural and social maladies? There's a case to be made for this. More than one, actually.

Rod Dreher, in *The Benedict Option: A Strategy for Christians in a Post-Christian Nation,*[1] offers one. I, in *Benedictine Options: Learning to Live from the Sons and Daughters of Saints Benedict and Scholastica*, offer another. Neither of us is a monastic.

Our proposals are fundamentally, even antithetically, different, but they both relate to the current moment.

People are fascinated by Benedictines. Magazines have feature stories on monasteries. Books on monastic spirituality fly off the shelves. We are at a time of extraordinary possibility for interchange between monastic tradition and the larger culture.

Rod Dreher and I are poles apart in what we see happening at that junction.

Dreher takes his cue from the conclusion of Alasdair MacIntyre's 1981 book, *After Virtue*: the world awaits "another—doubtless very different—St. Benedict."[2]

Dreher purports to introduce readers to people he calls "today's Benedicts." He credits traditionalists for still believing in "reason and virtue." Today's Benedicts are seeking "arks capable of carrying them and the living faith across the sea of crisis—a Dark Age that could last centuries."[3]

Throughout Dreher's book there are declarations about what the Benedict option is and what it isn't. Mostly he says that it's enough just for the faithful remnant to make it through the Dark Age unscathed. He eschews both "an imagined golden age" and "communities of the pure, cut off from the real world." But then he declares the Benedict option aims to reclaim "the real world from the artifice, alienation, and atomization of modern life."[4]

I, like Dreher, was captivated by MacIntyre's vision of a new Benedict. Like Dreher, I am all for "reason and virtue" and the flourishing of "the living faith." However, I see these being demonstrated not by his Benedicts sailing "across the sea of crisis," but by the Benedictines I have lived close to for almost half a century. Benedictine options are embodied in the *lives*—not just the life—of Benedictine men and women, who are not forsaking the world but are for the sake of the world.

The ark is a vivid and compelling picture for the Benedict option—the boat built by Noah to ride out the flood. My alternative image for Benedictine options is less precise, less circumscribed, but that is part of its point.

A participant in a 1989 conference I helped plan said that "we are in a saltwater marsh, where there is constant motion, teeming life, and an ever-shifting boundary between sea and land. Our task is . . . to notice what is going on all around us."[5] We are knee-deep in the marsh, not floating above it.

From Benedictines themselves I have learned to see the saltwater marsh world itself in many colors—indeed, into the spiritual infrared and ultraviolet. Dreher, on the contrary, sees the world as "growing cold, dead, and dark."[6]

Both Dreher and I look to Benedict as a guide for living in these days. I believe Benedictine options are a more authentic, more life-giving, and, actually, more *traditional* instruction than the Benedict option.

Benedictine options do not carry us across a sea of crisis. They are both a clue to what sort of place the world is and a prescription for reason and virtue and living faith in that world. I invite you to join me and Benedictines I know in an adventure in the marsh—an exploration of how to live.

"Turning His Back" and "His Spirit's Enlargement"

Pope Saint Gregory the Great's biography of Benedict, written several decades after the fact and based on interviews with some of Benedict's disciples, provides two stunningly disparate starting points for Dreher and me.

Here's Dreher: "Gregory writes that young Benedict was so shocked and disgusted by the vice and corruption in the city that he turned his back on the life of privilege that awaited him there, as the son of a government official. He moved to the nearby forest and later to a cave forty miles to the east. There Benedict lived a life of prayer and contemplation as a hermit for three years."[7]

Benedict's move that gets Dreher's attention is "turning his back." (It should be noted that after three years in the cave, Benedict went up a mountain and founded his monastery there.)

I begin elsewhere in Gregory's *Second Dialogue*: "According to [Benedict's] own description, the whole world was gathered up before his eyes in what appeared to be a single ray of light. . . . Of course, in saying that the world was gathered up before his eyes I do not mean that heaven and earth grew small, but that his spirit was enlarged. Absorbed as he was in God, it was now easy for him to see all that lay beneath God."[8]

Benedict's move that gets my attention is "his spirit's enlargement." I think it unlikely that when he saw "all that lay beneath God," Benedict spotted only vice and corruption.

So, Dreher and I have different sixth-century springboards— "turning his back" and "his spirit's enlargement."

Equally significant is the difference in where we look for evidence, especially contemporary evidence.

Dreher introduces us to some contemporary monks—sixteen of them—but they are all in one place, the Monastery of Saint Benedict in Norcia, Italy, Benedict's hometown. The monastery there was founded four centuries after Benedict's time, was suppressed by Napoleon in 1810, reopened in 2000, and is being reconstructed following a devastating earthquake in 2016. Its life today, with prayers in Latin and the pre-Vatican II Mass, is only one of many Benedictine options, and an uncommon one at that.

The independence of monasteries means that if you've seen one, you haven't seen them all. Even if you had seen all the men's monasteries, you'd have seen only half the evidence.

Among the 476 entries in the index to *The Benedict Option*, "monks" appear fourteen times, but there is no entry at all for "sisters (or nuns)." (The term "nun," which Dreher uses periodically in his text to refer to female Benedictines, is technical—it means a cloistered female monastic, which nearly all female Benedictines aren't. Throughout this book I will employ the term "sister," which Dreher doesn't use at all when referring to them.) There are about two dozen names of women, nearly all of them contemporary American evangelicals who are exemplars of life according to Dreher's "Benedict option."

There is no name of a living female Benedictine (and just one dead one: Benedict's twin sister, Scholastica). "Nuns" in other than a generic sense appear once in the book, but only as accompanying monks in prayer following the earthquake.[9] A book called *The Benedict Option* that includes in its index under "C" the archconservative archbishop emeritus of Philadelphia, Charles Chaput, but has no reference to Joan Chittister, OSB, is missing some options.

In other words, apart from a few men in Norcia, actual Benedictines are quite AWOL from *The Benedict Option*. This leaves Dreher free to read the Rule pretty much as he wants to.

Benedictine Options looks to the sons and daughters of Benedict and Scholastica for signals of the life-enhancing and world-affirming possibilities in lives lived according to their reading of the Rule. I have read a great deal about Benedictine monasticism, but my most important and formative research has been my more than four decades spent in the company of monastic people.

"How Does a Person Get To Be that Way?"

I had an "aha!" moment in 1989 when reading a *New Yorker* story by Jamaica Kincaid. The unnamed protagonist wonders about someone else, "How does a person get to be that way?"[10] I realized instantly: this is what drives my curiosity and research. It's the scholar's fundamental question: How does the person, virus, cosmos, institution, society, poem, language, statue, statute—whatever it is I am studying—get to be the way it is?

One of my conclusions is that the question has to be asked about every Benedictine individually—there is no one "way" that they are. There are many options.

Dreher's chapter 2, "A Rule for Living," drawing exclusively on his interviews with the monks of Norcia, makes many points with which I agree. But he situates them in sharp opposition to his portrayal of the modern world: "There is no middle ground."[11]

When there's no middle ground, there's of course only one Benedict option.

I do not believe the modern world is outer darkness; there's lots of middle ground. Benedictines have known many "modern worlds" during their millennium and a half. The unexpected doesn't throw them off course. The Rule has guided them steadily through the rise and fall of cultures. Because they have seen the waxing and waning of "modern world" after "modern world," they are skeptical both of Dr. Pangloss's contention that this is the best of all possible worlds and of Chicken Little's warning that the sky is falling. And some of them experience their entry into monastic life not as an escape, but as their chance to bring into the monastery the positive wisdom they have gained from their life in "the world." It is both/and, not either/or.

I have another disagreement with Dreher that is equally fundamental. He writes of "the religious model of the human person."[12] Just as I think there are many Benedictine options, so I think there are many religious *models* of the human person. This I have learned from, among others, Benedictines.

Dreher quotes, with evident approval, Father Cassian, prior of the Monastery of Saint Benedict in Norcia, talking about the reception of guests. " 'It's both that we reject what is not life-giving, and that we build something new. And we spend a lot of time in the rebuilding, and people see that too, which is why people flock to the monastery. . . . We are rebuilding. That's the *yes* that people have to hear about.' "

Here is how Dreher interprets what he heard: They "saw themselves as working on the restoration of Christian belief and Christian culture. How very Benedictine."[13]

There is a big difference between "restoration" and "rebuilding." I'm reminded of aphorisms by two of the greatest historians of Christianity. Adolph Harnack wrote, inviting restoration, "No religion gains anything through time; it only loses."[14] Saint John Henry Newman wrote, inviting rebuilding, "In a higher world it is otherwise, but here below to live is to change, and to be perfect is to have changed often."[15]

The Benedict Option is about restoration. *Benedictine Options* is about rebuilding. These are not the same thing.

chapter one

Where the Benedictine Charism *Isn't*

A leading feature of Benedict's Rule is its rootedness in the particular. The Rule is not some abstract theory devised by leisured academics in a seminar room. Benedict looks around him, says "Here we are," and asks, "What shall we do?"

The same question is posed to me as I start this book. Here we are, you and I. What shall we do?

And from the very beginning I need to put up "Danger" signs.

You, the reader, have every reason to expect me to say *what* the Benedictine charism is.

Charism is not an everyday word. In theology-speak, it's gift, a spiritual gift, even a gift of the Spirit. If you wonder what gift Benedictines are given by the Spirit, a gift they then in turn give to the rest of us, I have to tell you: It's much easier to say what it isn't than what it is.

To get even close to the *what*—close is the very most we can hope for—it's necessary to stake out the *what not*.

Danger Sign One: Definition Itself

If asked to define the Benedictine charism, I am in a position like that of Rabbi Hillel, an older contemporary of Jesus, who was challenged to teach the whole Torah while his listener stood on one foot. Hillel pronounced a form of what we know as the Golden

Rule, and said, "This is the whole of the Torah; the rest is the explanation of it. Go, learn it."[1] Hillel could get away with this brevity because of the authority he had gathered to himself through a lifetime of total immersion in the study and living of Torah.

If I were a monk, which I'm not, and a fifty-year jubilarian besides—I've lived close to Benedictines and worked with them for a half century, but it's not the same—I might venture a concise summary of the Benedictine charism. The summary would be complete and authentic, however, only if I added a warning: "Do not repeat what I said, for the charism resists all imposition by one on another." T. S. Eliot's lines suggest what it takes to be authentically succinct: "Quick now, here, now, always—/A condition of complete simplicity/(Costing not less than everything)."[2] Hillel made the same point: "Go, learn it."

Danger Sign Two: Presentism

"Of all the prejudices of pundits, presentism is the strongest. It is the assumption that what is happening now is going to keep on happening, without anything happening to stop it."[3]

You might think that these words of *New Yorker* writer Adam Gopnik have nothing to do with Benedictinism. Surely there is no group of people on Earth who are more attuned to the past. "Presentism" is the last prejudice they'd be guilty of.

But it's not the Benedictines I'm worried about here. It's us, those who are formed by the well-attested and much studied American historical amnesia.

It would be easy to conclude that monks and sisters are fossils from an ancient Yesterday. Today they are only a shadow. Tomorrow they will hardly be even a memory. They did us some good a long time ago, copying all those manuscripts and, more recently, teaching all those kids in parochial schools, tending all those patients in hospitals. Even now they can get a laugh on TV or the stage or in movies. But the world of microchips has no place for quill pens.

When I challenge presentism and futurism as the frame of reference, I do not mean that the Benedictine charism is the preserve of antiquarians. Quite the contrary: a concern for today and tomorrow is thoroughly Benedictine, but only when yesterday is given a voice.

G. K. Chesterton said it well: "Tradition means giving votes to the most obscure of all classes, our ancestors. It is the democracy of the dead."[4] It's "votes," not "a vote"—our ancestors aren't a monolith broadcasting a monologue. Benedictines know that the past is full of wise teachers, not all of whom teach the same thing—and some teachers thought wise in their own time turn out not to be, and vice versa. We are not left to figure out everything for ourselves, from scratch. When Yesterday is seen in its full sweep, it widens the scope of Today and deepens the horizon of Tomorrow.

Danger Sign Three: Snapshot

The first danger sign is definition, the second presentism. The third is the attempt to stop the motion.

There is no way I can account, in advance, for the fact that between this chapter and the end of the book I, as writer, and you, as reader, will become different. The very understanding of the Benedictine charism changes the one who is attempting to understand it. As Benedict says in the Rule (73.8), we're all at the beginning—all the time.

Avoiding the Dangers

To avoid the first danger, of definition, I am not going to define, at least in the usual academic sense. The Benedictine charism, like God in the fine title of a book by Samuel Terrien, is an "elusive presence."[5]

If I sidestep the first danger, defining, by not defining, I evade the second danger, neglect of the past, by retrieving it—selectively, of course—but not just the nearly two millennia that constitute the past of Christian monasticism.

Everyone reading this book has a past—some have more past than others. Part of the genius of the Benedictine charism is its linking our own pasts to our todays and tomorrows, and to the yesterday and today and tomorrow of the entire monastic community—indeed, of the whole world that Benedict saw gathered up into a single ray of light.

I do not know your past, you do not know mine. I will say a few things about mine. I hope this will inspire you to reflect on some features of your own past that might cast light, maybe from an unfamiliar or unexpected angle, on the Benedictine charism.

Finally, if I escape the trap of definition, and if I give voice to a past that gets drowned out in our American rush for "relevance" and "the latest thing," how can I skirt the third mistake— the preempting by this book of the changes it works in me while writing and in you while reading?

There's probably no way *around* this danger. *Through* it—that is, by my publishing the book and your opening it—is the only option. There is no sharp distinction between preliminaries and the real stuff. We are in the middle of things all the time.

My favorite book as a child—it is still my favorite book—Dr. Seuss's *The 500 Hats of Bartholomew Cubbins*, ends, "They only could say it just 'happened to happen' and was not very likely to happen again."[6] I think no poem has a better conclusion than the question of Keats's "Ode to a Nightingale": "Do I wake or sleep?" My endings are not in the league of Keats and Seuss, but they have set the standard I strive for.

Now that I have told you about endings, I am ready to face the question: "How shall I begin?"

"Where" and "How"

There is an obvious answer: start with the Rule. I did start with it, at least with one of its characteristics: its rootedness in the particular. But the Rule is not the proper starting point for the Benedictine charism; it is, rather, a point of reference.

One reason the Rule lives today, in a world vastly different from the one in which it was written, is that Benedict does not let any day—whether yesterday or today or tomorrow—tyrannize over any other day. Reflecting an assumption all but universal until the past couple of centuries, he considered the present in which he lived to be a serious decline from the golden age of the past.

Nevertheless, Benedict contents himself with a mild rebuke of the laxity of his contemporaries, and then establishes a context in which a life can grow. When we hear "rule" we think of regulations, strictures, "thou shalt nots." What Benedict constructs is more like a trellis. A plant climbing a trellis is finding its own path, within a framework; its space for movement is open, but not without boundaries. You cannot tell in advance just what way the branch will go.[7] And Benedict is explicit about this. Referring to the order of psalmody he has prescribed in careful and minute detail, he establishes a principle that can be applied to much else besides: if someone can think of a better arrangement, the change should by all means be made (18.22). Benedictines take their bearings from the Rule, but the Rule does not define their charism. To look for the charism in the Rule is to mistake the map for the territory.

My initial question resolves itself into two: "*Where* the Benedictine charism *isn't*," and "*How* the Benedictine charism *is*." I have avoided the pronoun "what" in favor of two adverbs: "where" it isn't and "how" it is.

The Benedictine charism is a rare bird. We must sneak up on it if we want to see it. At best, I suspect, we will catch a glimpse as it spreads its wings and takes off.

To consider where the Benedictine charism isn't is not to do anything new. Benedict himself had to ask the question. Lying close at hand in the early sixth century were the results of two hundred years of monastic experience, everything from elaborately organized communities of thousands of persons to pillar saints who lived alone atop columns, some of them four decades or more.

Benedict proposed a moderate form of monastic life. In so doing, he laid himself and his monks open to the charge of "cheapening" or "abandoning" "real" monasticism. Benedict would not have been at all surprised by the widespread plea, heard in recent years even in very high places, that sisters get back in the habit so as to be "real" sisters. He probably wouldn't have been surprised either at the catalogue of efforts over the centuries to reform Benedictinism itself (for example, the Cluniacs, the Cistercians, and the Trappists).

We have to consider the question where the Benedictine charism isn't, because there are many people who would project onto monks and sisters their own image of monasticism. They find the Benedictine charism a handy receptacle into which they can deposit for recycling their own ideals and/or frustrations. Benedictines must not take their cues from the pathologies, paranoias, prejudices, or purposes of others. They need to be wary lest others admire them to death.

I see three places where the Benedictine charism is not: 1) another world, either hell or heaven; 2) two "simplys"; and 3) the church, if we think the charism is a task.

Another World: Hell

In some regions of the popular mind there lurks a suspicion that the monastic life is a species of spiritual affliction caught in the lines of William Blake, "And priests in black gowns, were walking their rounds,/ And binding with briars, my joys & desires."[8] I doubt anyone enters the novitiate desiring a bound and blighted life, but if the twentieth-century psychological revolution has taught us anything—or, rather, has retrieved for us a truth that the early monastics knew—it has given us a healthy suspicion of our own motives.

The monastic life might beckon to some people because the prospect of stripped pleasures satisfies their inarticulate sense of unworthiness. The monastic life might beckon to some people because the anticipation of restricted opportunities relieves their dread of failure in the rough and tumble of the outside, everyday world. Someone whose will is unruly may secretly long for the abdication of will in favor of obedience to a superior, and count on the monastic system to establish psychological and moral limits hitherto not set by either nature or nurture.

Sometimes I am alarmed when I hear about the extensive use of psychological tests as part of the winnowing process for Benedictine candidates and novices. Such devices can seem like a technological invasion of territory that belongs to intuition, hunch, and discernment. But such tests can unmask, both for the community and for the candidate or novice, a twisted search for hell as a venue for salvation. There are, to be sure, very bad reasons to want to become a Benedictine. It is one thing—a good thing—to undertake a life of repentance. It is another thing—a bad thing—to hanker after a penitential life.

But the Benedictine charism is not just not hell on earth. It is, as well, not an obsessive concern with one's motives.

Our culture is caught in the crossfire between the value of spontaneity and the suspicion of motives. We catch ourselves watching ourselves and watch ourselves catching ourselves watching ourselves, spiraling into a kind of spiritual paralysis. Many people suspect that physical pleasures, disconnected from spiritual commitments, offer the only occasions for spontaneous experience.

Into the midst of all this convoluted confusion comes the Benedictine charism with a simple, even wry word, like that of a commercial some years back in the ongoing warfare between long-distance telephone companies: a representative of US Sprint says "Come on, AT&T, lighten up." We may expect the Benedictine charism to be heavy-handed, but it turns out, when we are hardest on ourselves, to be lighthearted. One could object that here I am putting the charism in conflict with the Rule, for the Rule is hardly a handbook for comedy. I would not be surprised, however, to discover an ancient manuscript of the Rule with a 74th chapter: "That every monk or sister should be a jester to every other."

Another World: Heaven

So, the Benedictine charism isn't finding a haven in hell. But it isn't the forecourt of heaven either.

Monastic lore is full of references to the monastic life as "the angelic life." There have been many periods in the church's history when it was assumed, probably more widely outside monasteries than within them, that the Rule is a blueprint, if not for heaven itself, at least for an embassy of heaven in the midst of the world.

To get a sense of how bizarre this notion is, consider the image, all too common, of the enclave of American diplomats or business people in some foreign country, re-creating in comically inappropriate environments the details of American suburban life, flying in familiar foods, and generally committing the vast pretense that the different world outside the compound does not really exist, or if it exists, is of no concern to them. We know how ineffective, even counterproductive, such behavior is, how deeply it builds resentment. If God has anything at all to do with the world and with monasticism, and further, if God is smart, the monastery will not be such an isolated, sealed-off outpost of heaven.

I doubt anyone thought entry into the monastery amounts to energizing a transporter in the fashion of *Star Trek* that will transfer a person instantaneously from the realm of earth to the realm of heaven. I would not be surprised, however, if some have at times hoped the monastery would be a buffer between them and the chances and changes of this mortal life, a bit of a breather from history that too often seems "one damned thing after another."

I know of no better way to disabuse oneself of the "monastery-as-isolated" illusion than to read the *Chronicles of Brother Cadfael*, the twenty-one engaging mystery novels of Ellis Peters. Brother Cadfael is a twelfth-century Benedictine herbalist who enters the monastery relatively late in life after some swashbuckling adventures in the Crusades. He and the entire monastic community of which he is a part are so intricately linked to the life of the surrounding communities that you realize the monastery wall, far from being an impenetrable barrier, is a thoroughly permeable membrane. In some ways life inside the monastery is more "worldly" than that outside, since there is, if not less deceit inside than outside, at least more honesty about the deceit.

As a recent commentator on Benedictine life has said, monks tend to be "gruffly honest" with each other.[9] The world outside the walls is full of schemes that will make everything right—in T. S. Eliot's mocking phrase, people "dreaming of systems so perfect that no one will need to be good."[10] In fact, there are more illusions of heaven on earth outside monasteries than within them. Benedict knows that the most we can hope for in this life is a good start. The Rule, he says, is a guidebook for beginners (73.8); it is not a prescription for a new world order.

When I deny that the monastery is either the atrium of hell or the antechamber to heaven, I am saying that the Benedictine charism is not a complete answer to life's questions, not even much of an answer at all. Benedictine life does not ease our fears of unworthiness by offering penances equal to our grievous faults; it does not fulfill our hopes of God's promises of a new heaven and new earth, or even of a restored Garden of Eden.

When we want punishment, the Benedictine charism tells us to lighten up. When we want to forsake the world, the charism tells us we are for the sake of the world. You may come to the monastery expecting a true/false test, or at least a multiple-choice one. What you find is an open-book essay exam, with a lifetime limit. To keep you guessing, the syllabus tells you it is only an introductory course.

Two "Simplys"

We have eliminated hell below and heaven above from the domain of the Benedictine charism. This leaves the world in the middle.

But the world is a various place, topsy-turvy, full of peril and promise, of innuendo and surprise. Lewis Carroll knew that to see the world clearly you sometimes have to go through the looking glass. It is a world of Catch-22s, a world in which a woman, in the TV show "Twin Peaks" not so long ago, listens to a log and eventually comes to seem almost normal. An apt image for our time is the menu of streaming choices available to anyone with a smartphone: from "Meet the Press" to "Saturday Night Live," from "American Gladiators" to "Mister Rogers' Neighborhood"—and all of which can be fast forwarded.

In the midst of such dizzying variety it is enormously tempting to say the Benedictine charism is simply somewhere or other. Simplicity is, without question, a Benedictine value, but simplicity is a noun and simply is an adverb. The two words function very differently. There are two claims often made about Benedictine life as being found simply somewhere, two claims that on first hearing seem attractive, plausible, even unexceptionable, but claims I want to challenge.

Not "Simply the Gospel"

The first of these "simplys" is this: Benedictine life is simply found in the gospel. Who could quarrel with that? "The gospel life" is no small claim, but it sounds smaller than "the angelic life." It seems to avoid the appearance of arrogating to oneself a status higher than that of other Christians. "You Benedictines must think of yourselves as better than the rest of us," an outsider might say. "Oh, no, we are just living the gospel life, as all Christians try to do. Please don't think we think we're better than you are!"

The Benedictine charism is not a call to a higher form of life. Disclaiming any such status is an essential feature of Benedictine identity. But to ground that disclaimer in the notion that Benedictine life is "simply the gospel life" is a serious mistake, for at least two reasons.

It is a mistake, first of all, because Martin Luther was right when he insisted that there are many ways to live the gospel life, none of them intrinsically superior to the others. Luther directed furious invective against monasticism—for him, the ex-monk, monasticism was, in a way, a god that failed, hence his bitterness—but the monastic life, minus any claim that it was a particularly pure form of the gospel life, could find a theoretical home in Luther's world, and is these days finding a practical nest in some branches of the tree Luther planted—"Protestant monasticism" is growing in many places.[11] If I come to you and say I am simply living the gospel life, I may have no thought of lording it over you—it may be a genuinely humble observation on my part—but you will not hear it that way.

To say that the Benedictine charism is simply the gospel life is to claim, even unintentionally, too much. But it also claims too little. If a sister or monk comes to me and says, "I am simply living the gospel life," I will feel both demeaned and disappointed: demeaned because "I thought it was possible simply to live the gospel in my way of life"; disappointed because "I want your form of life to challenge my life, not call it into question or undermine it."

In other words, I want you to say: "My Benedictine way of living the gospel life—a very particular, even a very peculiar, way of living it—illustrates some values that you could express in your life too. I am not simply living the gospel life. I have chosen a way of being Christian that suits me, but certainly does not suit everyone—sometimes, frankly, truth be told, I wonder anew if it suits me. It is a form of life as full of pitfalls, as subject to corruption, as sad and funny as any other. Like all forms of Christian life, it stands at all times under the judgment of the gospel."

I want you to say these things because I believe no one lives, or should even intend to live, "simply the gospel life." The gospel life is not an individual matter; the gospel is lived by a community, a body in which eyes don't try to function like feet, or hands like ears. The Benedictine charism is a function, one among many, carried out by some members of the Body of Christ. It is part of the gospel life, but the gospel life is far vaster, richer, more many-splendored and deeply-shadowed, than any of us can manage on our own. "Simply" and "the gospel life" do not belong in the same sentence.

Not "Simply Essential Humanity"

"Simply the gospel life" is not the only "simply" claim that is made for the Benedictine charism.

There is another, even more general claim that is voiced with increasing frequency: the Benedictine charism is found simply in "essential humanity." This is an enormously appealing claim, one I consider actually more plausible than "simply the gospel life." There is a wisdom, a sanity, a clarity in the Rule that speaks in accents resonant with much other wisdom that has been distilled from cultural experiences remote from Christian monasticism.

It is no accident that Benedictine monks and sisters have a kind of instinctive affinity with monastics from other traditions, and an openness to insight, whatever its pedigree. The peculiarly Christian language of humility in the Rule raises barriers on first reading to some who are unfamiliar with it, but when humility is understood in its basic meaning—an honest, ungrudging acknowledgment and acceptance of who one is—it becomes accessible across religious traditions and cultural barriers, a value that unites.

Still, attractive and laudable—and largely legitimate—as is the claim that the Benedictine charism is simply essential humanity, I believe that "simply essential humanity" is properly in the category "Where the Benedictine charism isn't." Just as the Benedictine charism is one way among many of being Christian, it is a Christian way, among many other ways both Christian and non-Christian, of being human.

I touch here on an ancient theological debate that has taken on new urgency in our tightly interconnected world: universalism and particularism in Christianity.

I will deal with this question at greater length when discussing Monastic Interreligious Dialogue in chapter 6, but will say now that I believe there are strong similarities, deep affinities between the great religious traditions—more in common than most of our ancestors thought. I am not talking about a least common denominator; I take my cue from C. S. Lewis that "those who are at the heart" of their different traditions "are all closer to one another than those who are at the fringes."[12] If the Benedictine charism is not "simply Christian," it is not "simply essential humanity" either.

Not the Church

First, then, in the category of another world, I have ruled out hell or heaven. Second, on the plane of this world, I have ruled out "simply the gospel" or "simply essential humanity." The third and last of my three places not to look for the Benedictine charism is the church.

Of course, I do not mean there is no connection to the church. There could not be a more vivid dramatization of the link between the charism and the church than the newly professed monk's or sister's placing the signed vow on the altar during the profession ceremony, a procedure explicitly mandated in the Rule (58.20). But such a link does not make a charism, even if the church for a long time insisted that it does.

Monasteries have characteristically paid only as much attention to ecclesiastical edicts as they have wanted to. A monk once answered my query, "What do you do when the bishop sends you a directive that you don't like?" "We post it on the bulletin board." I imagine many a US president and many a diocesan bishop would nod knowingly when the one talked about dealing with Congress or the other about dealing with monasteries.

But despite their much prized independence, monasteries, especially in the United States, and more especially monasteries of women, have over time let ecclesiastical officials define their charism in terms of ecclesiastical tasks. Waking up to this fact creates tensions, and initiates in monastic communities sharp debates over their very identity.

My ruling out hell, heaven, "simply the gospel," and "simply essential humanity" may hit some Benedictines directly, but others may feel the categories a little remote, too academic. To rule out the church is to hit close to home. I might be said to have quit describing and started meddling.

The issue presents itself differently in monasteries of men and in those of women.

The Church's Tasks

In theory the line between monk and priest is clear, and "monk" takes priority. "If any ordained priest asks to be received into the monastery, do not agree too quickly. However, if he is fully persistent in his request, he must recognize that he will have to observe the full discipline of the rule without any mitigation" (60.1-3). Benedict's language here suggests strongly that he suspected this ordering was precarious, as it turned out to be. The hierarchy of "fathers" and "brothers" bedeviled monasteries for centuries until more recently, in the aftermath of the Second Vatican Council.

Monasteries of men are godsends for bishops who need a large supply of clergy. It is sometimes difficult to detect any difference between the life of a monastic priest and that of a diocesan priest, especially when the monk's assignment is far away from the monastery. Now and then the chance to assign a particularly troublesome monk to a distant parish may be a boon for the abbot, but such an assignment could be too easy an evasion of the sort of tough decisions that the Rule expects will occasionally have to be made. Of course, not all monks are priests, and there are other ecclesiastical tasks the ordained do besides sacramental ones, but the tension between priestly and monastic identity is a perennial question in men's monastic communities.

For the foreseeable future, women Benedictines will not have an opportunity to confront the anomaly inherent in the mishmash of monastic identity and priestly identity. That "foreseeable future," according to the late cardinal archbishop of Philadelphia, Anthony Bevilacqua, is very long: "Not in a hundred, not in a thousand, not in a million years" will women be priests.[13] If and when ordination becomes an option for them, they will need to be wary of the danger to monastic identity itself, the potential dissonance with the Benedictine charism.

While the church has not assigned sisters the task of celebrating the Eucharist, it has not thereby left them to their own devices. The tally of apostolic services performed in and for the church by Benedictine sisters is staggering, all the more because they have done so little to blow their own trumpet.

I do not begin to know all the kinds of things that have been accomplished; the ones I hear about most are teaching and nursing. I doubt there is any part of the church's activity, apart from the exclusively priestly, that does not have a significant Benedictine women's stamp on it.

This is a blessing for the church. It is to the undying credit of the sisters. But it is not the Benedictine charism. There are apostolic orders by the scores or hundreds; their mission, their self-understanding, is to do the jobs the church, in the person of the bishop, asks them to do. This is not what Benedictines are for.

But it is comforting to think it is what they are for. There is a good fit between apostolic responsibility and American values:

we are a people who do things, assign tasks, set goals. We like to be able to say, at the end of a day or an assignment or a lifetime, that we have done what we set out to do. An apostolic task—such as a class to teach, blood pressures to check, Mass to celebrate—gives a chance to say "I have done it." Such assignments even give a chance to say "I have not done it"—sometimes students do not learn, patients die, homilies fall flat—but knowing we have failed is at least definite knowledge.

The real problem—the real terror—of acknowledging that the Benedictine charism is not an ecclesiastical task is the inescapable recognition that the charism does not fit with our American pragmatic ideal. If it is not a task, how will we know we have done it? How, even, will we know we have not done it? Is the hunt for the Benedictine charism, to use an image proposed by my Oxford tutor in a different context, "groping blindfold for absent black cats in darkened rooms"?[14] Anything, you may say—give us anything except this emptiness.

This is a suitably precarious place to leave the question of definition, of where the Benedictine charism isn't.

Heaven and hell won't do. The gospel and essential humanity won't do. Not even the church will do. What will?

Another adverb: *How?*

chapter two

How the Benedictine Charism *Is*

First, a quick recap of the previous chapter—and by the time I've done with this one, you will see that we'll be looking again where I said we shouldn't look at all.

I do not want to disconnect the charism from the intricate and intimate networks of history and of our common life.

You, the reader, and I are tied—inextricably, even if by rejection—to notions of hell and heaven, or at least to notions that have traditionally been phrased in those terms.

You, the reader, whether Christian or not, and I have ideas of the gospel and essential humanity that are bound to shape our understanding of the Benedictine charism—of just about everything else in our experience, for that matter.

I, and maybe (or maybe not) you, the reader, feel an obligation to the church and its tasks, and the Benedictine charism cannot be sealed off from all contact with this sense of obligation.

I said, and say again, those are not the places to look for the Benedictine charism. But once we have found out "how" it is even if "what" it is continues to elude us, then we can return to those places—hell, heaven, the "simplys," and the church—and detect the links, the resonances. We can reconnect with the full reach of God's creation.

No Answer to "What?"

I have modified, then, slightly, my insistence that the Benedictine charism cannot be found where we might most readily have thought to look for it. But I remain convinced of the impossibility of saying "what" the charism is.

Many answers have been offered to the question, "What is the Benedictine charism?" The Rule says to prefer nothing to the Work of God and to prefer nothing to Christ. To say that one's charism is to prefer nothing to Christ is profound, but also obscure. To say that one's charism is to prefer nothing to the Work of God is more specific—Benedictines are, after all, more scrupulous, not to say more obsessive, than most people about praying, particularly praying the psalms. But praying is only part of what they do.

More precise still is the claim that the Benedictine charism is community, with its close corollary, hospitality. But even this answer to the "What?" is unsatisfactory, because there are other models of community, and among Benedictines there is no single design.

I have never heard an answer to the "What?" that I think gets it right. But that there is an "it" I believe to be indisputable. People who spend time at the place where I worked for twenty years, the Collegeville Institute for Ecumenical and Cultural Research, report almost without exception their overwhelming sense of the Benedictine presence of Saint John's Abbey and University, and Saint Benedict's Monastery and the College of Saint Benedict. They also admit a frustration similar to mine when they try to account for it when talking to other people.

I have concluded, after puzzling for many years over the way Benedictine reality resists classification, that the charism is no one thing. It is not even a collection of things.

It is a way things are done, a way comprised of several characteristics that are in constantly shifting relationship to each other—a kaleidoscope, not a formula. I catch glimpses of these components now and then, but the kaleidoscope keeps turning and the pattern changes. The closest I will come to defining the charism is to say it is the kaleidoscope itself, not any of the momentary designs the kaleidoscope happens to display.

I will talk about "how" the charism is rather than "what" it is. The "how" implies a "what," but indirectly.

Five Answers to "How?"

None of these five answers is adequate by itself. Even the full assemblage of these five does not tell exhaustively how the charism is. But if you come across something that has these five characteristics, in whatever proportions, you might want to wager that you have found a Benedictine charism. The five "hows" are these: experimental, rhythmical, communal, ecumenical, and narrational.

Experimental

You will sometimes hear it said that Benedictinism is an experiment in communal living that works. College courses about utopias may include a section on monasticism, but in that context monasticism is an anomaly, because all other utopian schemes have existed only in somebody's head, or, if the scheme has actually been tried, it has lasted at best a few generations.

The question then becomes, Why is the monastery a utopian experiment that works? The answer is that monasticism does not belong in a course on utopias at all, because it is not an experiment. It is, more than any other human enterprise known to me, genuinely experimental.

This may sound like a word game—making a sharp distinction between the noun experiment and the adjective experimental—but it is a game with major consequences.

The real agenda of every utopian proposal is a sharply etched portrayal of the human ideal. The experiment is designed to bring that ideal to full expression. The designer of a utopia knows exactly what the utopia will look like when it is completely realized, because the designer knows exactly what a perfect human being looks like.

The utopia—a laboratory for authoritarianism—is, in the most stringent sense, a *controlled* experiment. Rod Dreher's Benedict option appears to me to come perilously close to a utopian experiment—he writes of the replacement in America of "the religious model of the human person" by "a psychological model"[1]—*the* religious model, which the option aims to reassert.

The Benedictine understanding of community is utterly, almost comically, different from that of the utopian dreamer.

Benedict is so far from acknowledging a uniform pattern of human perfection that he puts the abbot under obligation to pay special attention to the idiosyncrasies of each monk (2.31-32). By insisting that the monastic life lived in full compliance with the Rule will amount to no more than a beginning in the search for God (73.8), Benedict abjures any claim to know what the community will look like when it reaches its goal. Benedictine life is experimental all the way to the end.

In short: the Rule of Benedict, gathering up and filtering the accumulated monastic experience of two centuries, manages one of the neatest tricks in the history of human organization. It codifies and regulates an experimental way of life—a way of life that is always open to new options.

The resolutely, irreducibly experimental character of the Benedictine charism has implications all along the way. It puts the midlife crisis into perspective. It gives space for the moments, or even the long stretches, when you are sure that if you don't leave the monastery you will go crazy. Because the life is experimental, if by God's grace you live to the golden jubilee of your profession you will on that occasion renew your vow in the same terms you used at the beginning.

So doing, you acknowledge that you are still in a school for the Lord's service, that you have yet much to learn, that the novice who comes to you expecting to discover that after half a century you have the answer may well be able to teach you more than you can teach her or him. An experimental life is not accidental, does not operate on whim—the Rule states a mission, to seek God—but is tentative about the means. "For now, in this place, with these people, we will do thus. But tomorrow is a new day, with different challenges."

For novices, the experimental character of the charism means the novitiate is not properly understood as an apprenticeship. Novices do not spend the initial years acquiring a skill for a particular job. They learn things, of course; they are even developing skills. But at the end of the novitiate they are not "ready" to "do" Benedictine life, to hang the "OSB" shingle over their shop.

It would no doubt be gratifying to have a clearly defined charism, one you can decide you have or have not fulfilled by checking boxes on a questionnaire—just as it has been gratifying for monks and sisters to have particular apostolic tasks assigned by the church, something you can do and know you have done.

But specific ecclesiastical tasks are not where the Benedictine charism is. Neither does the Benedictine charism stand or fall with the success or failure of a particular experiment. Novices have much, very much, to learn from their elders in the monastic life, but the wisest of those elders will let the newcomers know that there is no apprenticeship. *That* there is a Benedictine charism, the elder can demonstrate; *what* that charism is for the novice, the novice will have to figure out.

Because the Benedictine charism is experimental, when things go bad they don't go bust, since everyone in the monastery knows that some things will work and some things will not. Failure now and then is to be expected. At the moment it becomes a utopia a monastery would self-destruct.

Because the Benedictine charism is experimental, monastic life has an attractive ordinariness. If monks and sisters were engaged in an experiment, they would be deadly serious, anxious about many things, self-absorbed. But Benedictines, as I know them, anyway, are graced with a more immediate humor, make less grandiose claims for themselves, are more readily available to others than most people I know.

Of course, life in a monastery is not free of the pathologies of control, but curiously, while to the outsider the monastery might seem the embodiment of a controlled environment, it is in fact an uncommonly spontaneous place.

Rhythmical

This spontaneity is grounded not only in the experimental character of the Benedictine charism but also in the second of the answers to the "how": its rhythmical character.

This is a paradox. One would think a pattern of life that has set times for prayer every day would crush spontaneity. But the Rule itself is quite clear that prayer is to be balanced by work. Both are to be balanced by sleep. Benedict knew of the many forms of monastic extremism that had been tried in the previous two hundred years. He wanted none of it. But he knew, too, that left without pattern, the monastic search would be not spontaneous, but simply aimless, like the random wanderings of the gyrovagues: "Always on the move, they never settle down, and are slaves to their own wills and gross appetites" (1.11).

The rhythm of the Divine Office, the Work of God, is among the most striking characteristics of Benedictine life. It has been remarked on so often by so many practitioners and observers that I will take it as a given. I will concentrate on another rhythmical aspect of the charism, its linkage to the liturgical year.

The whole church has this connection. Even the most casual churchgoer is apt to notice the changes of vestment color. But there is in the monastery an attentiveness to the liturgical calendar that means the spiritual highs and lows of purple, white, red, and green penetrate the fibers of the soul.

The rich variety of the liturgical seasons reinforces the daily balanced diet of faith and doubt, hope and despair, love and hate, that every Benedictine gets from the psalms. The rhythmical character of the charism frees the Benedictine not to fear spiritual darkness or to be overly elated by spiritual light. Advent will be succeeded by Christmas/Epiphany, then Lent by Palm Sunday and Good Friday, Good Friday by Easter, Easter by Pentecost, and then Pentecost by Ordinary Time and Ordinary Time and Ordinary Time.

The rhythm of the liturgical year tells the Benedictine: we scale the heights and plumb the depths, but we do not glory in the zeniths or wallow in the abysses, nor do we succumb to boredom in the middle, for our confidence is not in our spiritual state but in the knowledge that all spiritual states are part of God's calendar.

I said earlier that I would connect some of my own past to the discussion of the Benedictine charism. These words, about spiritual heights and depths and how they are all within the divine geography, help me locate my father's death by suicide. I will never know in detail the nature of the anguish of his thoughts and feelings. I know he believed the demons had won. I believe he was mistaken.

The knowledge of God, even if only a secondhand knowledge, that I gain from the rhythmical character of the Benedictine charism helps ground my confidence that the demons' victory, while apparent, is only provisional. I wish my father could have known that. Maybe he knew it, in which case I wish he could have believed it. But what matters finally is not what he knew or didn't know, what he could or could not believe. What matters is the faithfulness of God, a faithfulness of which the rhythmical character of the Benedictine charism is a steady reminder.

Communal

I wish my father's despair had been relieved by the knowledge of God's faithfulness that is carried in the Benedictine charism. I wish further that his sense of isolation, of being unavailable to others and inaccessible by others, had been relieved by the third answer to the "how" of the charism, its communal character.

The Benedictine instinct for and experience of wisdom about community is probably its most widely recognized and often noted feature. As I noted in the introduction to Part One, Alasdair MacIntyre electrified both Rod Dreher and me when he concluded his analysis of the breakdown of effective community during the past couple of centuries by saying we are waiting for a new Saint Benedict.[2] I believe we still have much to learn from the old Saint Benedict. However, I look even more to those who have embarked on this life together to illustrate and expand those lessons for the rest of us.

The term community appears everywhere these days, on the right, on the left, and across the middle of social, political, ecclesiastical, economic, educational, psychological debates. Nearly everybody believes community is something we need more of, but there is nothing like consensus on what it is or how to get it.

Benedictinism—the Rule itself, the history of monasteries, including their decline and renewal, the development of constitutions and federations, and, most important, the stories monastics tell—all of this constitutes a cascade of wisdom and caution about community. Nonetheless, I resist identifying the Benedictine charism with community. That would be to say "what" it is. I have set out to say "how" it is: the charism is not community, but it is communal.

To the casual observer, the main thing Benedictines know about groups of people is that someone has to be in charge. The authority of the abbot and prioress is vast—they are, after all, in the place of Christ. Surely, then, the communal feature of the charism is at least equally balanced by its hierarchical character.

But someone's being in charge is not necessarily hierarchical. Communities that on ideological principle deny anyone is in charge do not last long. Community and responsibility are not incompatible; the issue is how responsibility is understood. The Benedictine charism is communal, without indulging in the naive nonsense that a body does not need a head.

The communal feature of the Benedictine charism expresses itself primarily in discernment, an activity that both energizes authority and restrains authority. Discernment is not the same as voting, or surveying by questionnaire, or even consensus. It gives room to imagination, now and then turns up a complete surprise.

Discernment requires patience far beyond what our culture, with its short attention span and its obsession with the quarterly report bottom line, is accustomed to. Discernment is not an activity of community building, but of community unfolding. The image of community building, so common in our speech these days, implies control, design, programs, as though people were a kind of inert bricks to be fitted into some architectural scheme.

The Benedictine charism is communal not like a blueprint or organization chart, but like a garden—an English garden, actually: "profusion and luxuriance . . . the extraordinary variety of plants—the flowering shrubs, the herbaceous perennials, the herbs, the annuals, the bulbs, the wild flowers, and the ground covers."[3]

Communal discernment has a paradoxical consequence. Many people are convinced that unless I do my thing and you do your thing neither of us is ourselves. They are wary of community for fear it will obliterate individuality. But discernment, because everyone is heard, helps to preserve, even enhance, individuality.

Of course, not everybody can have their own way. Some profound voices from Eastern Europe warned that unrestrained Western style individualism can be as destructive of humane values—actually, as destructive of true individuality—as was the stifling conformism demanded by the now discredited totalitarian systems. Individualism, as distinct from and even opposed to individuality, leads to the conviction that if the group's decision does not correspond to what I proposed, then I was not heard, because if I had been truly heard the rightness of my position would have been self-evident to everyone.

The habit of discernment presupposes no illusion that everyone will agree on a course of action, including my own most carefully crafted plan. The habit of discernment frees me to acknowledge better wisdom than my own—especially to expect that speaking and listening by everyone will result in a proposal better than any that was initially brought to the discussion by anyone. When something comes out of a meeting that no one came into it with, pay very close attention.

That Benedictines know much about community, certainly more than most people, I would not dispute for a minute. But there is a danger in thinking that the charism is community. Once monastics start thinking in those terms, they and those who admire them fix attention on structural details, so the question becomes one of organizational technology.

The charism is not about how to organize. It is about unlocking, unleashing, surprising. The Benedictine charism carries the notice "All Natural. Nothing Artificial. No Preservatives Added." The only preservative is the unflagging commitment to discernment itself. To trust that discernment is the key to survival is radical enough, but the Benedictine charism is bolder even than that. It trusts discernment is the key to flourishing as well.

A grand and tenacious faith undergirds the communal character of the Benedictine charism: a faith that the components of a true community are already present when people get together, that God has made us for community and given us what we need for it.

Benedictines do not figure out in advance how to get together. They assume God wants them together. Their job is to discern how, once they are together, they can be—each and every one of them—what God has made each and every one of them to be: not all the same. The Benedictine charism sets itself squarely against the cynicism captured in the crisp phrase of Thomas Hobbes, a phrase deeply embedded in our culture, that human life is by its nature "solitary, poor, nasty, brutish, and short."[4]

Ecumenical

Following on experimental, rhythmical, and communal, to name ecumenical as the fourth answer to "how" the Benedictine charism is might seem far-fetched. After all, the symbolic power of monasticism was close to the heart of the disputes of the Protestant Reformation that split the church in the sixteenth century. Surely, then, the Benedictine charism is peculiarly Roman Catholic, and should be kept in the background if we want progress toward Christian unity.

The historical fact of monasticism's divisiveness becomes a historical curiosity, however, in face of the key role played by monks and sisters in recent decades in the movement for Christian unity. There is something about the charism that responds to the magnetic pull of ecumenism. Monks and sisters cannot stay away.

The ecumenical nature of the charism evidences itself in several ways. Most important, I believe, is its lay character. Here, of course, women Benedictines are the norm. Benedict legislated for a community of laypersons and made grudging provision for priests in the monastery. Popular Catholic opinion may put monks and sisters in a category of holiness above the ranks of the laity, but I have a strong impression that much energy for monastic renewal in recent years has come from the determination among monastic people themselves to disclaim any such status.

The ecumenical movement of the twentieth century began as a primarily lay movement. Like so much else in the churches, ecumenism has been time and again taken over by the ordained, but laypersons have repeatedly asserted their claim to be the primary bearers of unity.

The monastery is an instructive example of an intensely religious life lived by non-ordained people. Ironically, the monastery is a better illustration of the priesthood of all believers than are many Protestant churches that give lip service to Luther's dictum but are in fact at least as riddled with deference to the ordained as is any Roman Catholic parish.

The Benedictine charism is ecumenical because it is lay. It is ecumenical also because it is, to a degree almost unparalleled in our society, intergenerational. There is something comical in the linguistic refinements our social engineers and journalists have fashioned to designate various age groups. One reason we have such a devilish time realizing any community is that very narrow bands in the generational spectrum have been persuaded that they have particular and peculiar interests that are at sharp odds with those of all the other bands.

Over and against this obsession with interests comes the Rule of Benedict with its almost offhand appreciation for the gifts each band has to offer the others. The old and the young and those across the middle are all to defer to each other (71.1). Rank in the monastery, such as it is, is to be determined solely by date of entry (63.1-8). I suspect such ranking was instituted mainly to avoid disputes about who would stand where when a procession had to be organized.

The overwhelming impression given by the Rule is that such ranking has little if any practical daily significance. The Benedictine intuition that the young, the newcomer, may have the word from God the community needs (3.3), is especially instructive these days. One of the sharpest confrontations at the 1991 World Council of Churches Assembly in Canberra, Australia, was generated by young delegates who, when the Council failed to give them adequate representation on the Central Committee, unfurled a banner proclaiming the lack of emphasis on youth participation as "Ecumenical Suicide."[5]

The lay character and intergenerational openness of the Benedictine charism are two of its ecumenical features. A third is harder to specify but is even more fundamental. The Benedictine charism models, quietly and therefore powerfully, identity without exclusion.

Benedictines, like any human being, have periods of doubt, sometimes of profound doubt, about their identity. In my observation, however, they are remarkably clear about who they are—clearer, at least, than most of us are about our identities. Because they know who they are, they are nondefensive. For just this reason they are remarkably available as counselors and friends to others who may be very different from them.

I once interviewed Father Columba Stewart, OSB, a monk of Saint John's Abbey and executive director of the Hill Museum & Manuscript Library, which has brought the medieval tradition of manuscript preservation into the digital age, including Muslim and Buddhist and Hindu holdings. He was preparing a lecture called "Cultural Heritage Present and Future: A Benedictine Monk's Long View."[6]

I asked him, "What accounts for this 'long view'?" "Being deeply rooted in a tradition," he responded, "we Benedictines are able to be confident in opening ourselves intellectually and ecumenically because we don't feel threatened by stuff that's newer. We're like a deep-rooted tree—we can sway a bit."[7]

Benedictines make judgments, of course, but they are among the least judgmental people I have ever encountered. There can be few truths more important for ecumenism than this: real availability to one another does not require a least-common-denominator reduction to some bland uniformity. On the contrary, those who, because their identity is secure, are not threatened by another who is different, can be truly open to the other. I can offer you my gifts only if I do not have to expend my energy in protecting my turf.

Narrational

The fifth and last of my answers to the question "*How* the Benedictine charism *is*" weaves the other four together. I choose this image deliberately. The portrayal of human interaction, including our speaking together, as "weaving" is among the most valuable lessons that feminism has taught me. When I resist the effort to define the Benedictine charism, I am acknowledging the feminist wisdom that the world may be more accurately reflected on a loom than on a piece of graph paper. A book about Benedictine women in Central Minnesota is called *Threads from Our Tapestry.*[8] This feminist wisdom is for the healing of all of us.

The fifth characteristic of the Benedictine charism, the one that weaves together the experimental, the rhythmical, the communal, and the ecumenical, is the narrational. The monastic life is in the stories monastics tell about their life—the stories they hear from those who have gone before, the ones they tell about each other, the ones they tell about themselves. The stories are not the raw material from which the charism can be precipitated out by some analytical catalyst. The story itself is where the universal and the unique, the concrete and the abstract, get connected.

During my first two years in college as an English history and literature major I functioned with a critical assumption that in retrospect is ludicrous, though at the time it seemed perfectly reasonable. I believed that poetry was a way of saying something that the poet would have said in straightforward prose had he or she been able to do so. In other words, poetry is what happens when you are unable to say what you really mean. My attempts at poetry criticism were efforts—I mean *efforts*—to plot a tapestry on graph paper.

My junior year Romantic Poetry teacher earned my lasting gratitude by skillfully leading me to the point at which, on reading Keats's "Ode to Autumn" and reaching the final line, "And gathering swallows twitter in the skies," I burst into uncontrollable tears. I was embarrassed—and freed forever from the rationalist delusion that poetry is frustrated prose.

The narrational character of the Benedictine charism is not reducible to some formula, translatable into some clear answer to "What is the Benedictine charism?" If someone asks a monk or sister what it means to be a Benedictine and he or she, properly, starts to tell a story, and the listener says "No, I don't want an anecdote, I want to know what it means," the only response is to continue the story or tell another one.

A friend of mine recounts a delicious Benedictine tale, a true one that by both its content and its form makes the point about the narrational character of the Benedictine charism.

She and a friend were on a vacation trip with a monk. They were in a pickup truck on a narrow dirt road, going up the side of a steep mountain. The monk was driving. The friend, terrified, decided to try to keep the monk's mind focused by asking questions about the monastic life.

"What is it that binds you monks together?" she asked, and then herself offered a series of options. The monk kept responding, "No, that's not required." Finally, in exasperation, she said, "But surely you all have to believe in God!" The monk thought briefly and then said, "Not really; there was that brother who lost his faith for all those years, but he was still part of the community." "Then isn't there *anything* you all have to be?" After a pause the monk said, "Yes: tolerant."

Recognizing that the Benedictine charism is fundamentally, irreducibly narrational has helped me understand an observation made by several sisters and monks, one that puzzled me when I first heard it. They have told me that the key to monastic renewal in recent decades has been the rediscovery of the habit of *lectio divina*. They do not find it easy to say just what *lectio divina* is. As you might expect, I take such imprecision to be a sign that they are talking about something really important.

The point as I understand it is this: reading, of Scripture and of other texts, is to be done in an experimental, rhythmical, communal, and ecumenical way, looking to weave the strands of meaning in the text into the reader's experience. You do not take time out from life to read. You realize that those who wrote were not taking time out from life to write. Writing and reading are both understood to be part of a narrative. The line between my personal narrative and the narrative of the community of which I am part begins to blur.

If Benedictine life depended on there being a clear-cut answer to the question, "What is the Benedictine charism?" the answer that would be least wrong is this: The Benedictine charism is *lectio divina*. If, in the tradition of Rabbi Hillel, the monastic then said, "Go, learn it," and the listener asked, "Where should I go?" here's a good suggestion: go to Saint Joseph, Minnesota, and listen to the bells in the library tower at the College of Saint Benedict.

There are four bells. The president of the college and the prioress of the monastery, with fine instinct, decided to name the bells *lectio, meditatio, oratio,* and *contemplatio*—the traditional stages of *lectio divina*. The bells ring every hour, reminding the hearer that the process of reading, meditating, praying, and contemplating is always going on, always starting over, always reaching its goal only to go back to the beginning. The bells can be heard throughout the campus and the town, reminding everyone that *lectio divina* is much more than reading books; it is a way of living. The bells tell the "how" of the charism.

part two

Tradition and Traditions

Tradition is often proposed as the cure for what ails us. However, tradition frequently poses more questions than it answers.

Fiddler on the Roof begins with the song "Tradition, Tradition." In this song, family and social and religious roles are clearly and humorously prescribed. The show has many themes. One is the necessity of tradition bending, even breaking, to preserve what tradition was supposed to protect in the first place. "To live," as Newman said, "is to change."

The word "tradition" (by itself and in "traditional" and "traditionalist") appears ninety-six times in *The Benedict Option*. The term turns up once in the index: "traditional, conservative" under the general category of "Christianity," tacitly disallowing that anything "liberal" might actually be "traditional" Christianity.

Dreher often precedes "tradition" with "the," applying it to Christian principles, Christian worldview, marriage and family, Western culture—implying that there's only one kind of each. Mainline Protestants, considered by Dreher to be also-rans ("cratering" is the image he uses), are faulted by him for ignorance of their own roots.[1]

Now, I won't take second place to Dreher as an advocate for knowledge of the past. I agree with him that Christians who

today "reject" the wisdom of past ages are thereby impover-
ished. I wouldn't put it snidely, as Dreher does—pitting the
fathers of the church against "the thin gruel of contemporary
Christianity"—but Christians long dead have left us rich nour-
ishment. Here is a motion of Dreher's that I happily second:
"When Christians ignore the story of how our fathers and mothers in the faith prayed, lived, and worshiped, we deny the life-
giving power of our own roots and cut ourselves off from the
wisdom of those whose minds were renewed."[2]

My problem is with "the" story. Dreher mentions not only
fathers in the faith but also mothers—of whom we know so
little. His phrase makes it sound as if they're on equal footing.

Yes, it is unfortunate that the study of the early church is
called "patristics"; but modifying it to include "matristics" is
pretty artificial—a Saint Helena and Saint Macrina and Saint
Scholastica and a handful of desert ammas are a notable bunch,
but are swamped in the male tide. Perhaps we should simply
call it "ancestristics."

Further, even those ancestors in the faith who have made it
through the "orthodoxy" filter are not all of one mind, and then
there are the ones who fell afoul of authorities—often political
authorities.

Dreher's traditionalist move that most constricts the Benedict option is his appeal to Western civilization. He claims that
without the Benedict option as he articulates it, "Western civilization" is doomed. If you want to know where Western civilization is, he tells us that it's in the tradition of the Great Books.

I join him in saluting medieval Benedictines for their role in
preserving many of the Great Books, including, of course, the
classics of Greece and Rome.[3] I dispute his claim that there is
something that can be delimited as "Western civilization." Further, I unite with feminists and other revisionists in insisting
that even the Great Books must be read between the lines,
through the looking glass, around the edges, listening for their
silences, in order to detect voices and realities that were filtered
out by the culture.

The most important virtue of Western civilization is its capacity for self-critique. It's not just Aristotle criticizing Plato. It's us criticizing both Plato and Aristotle for their male short-sightedness. Western civilization, to the extent that it's a reality, is both a life jacket and a straitjacket.

For Dreher, it's not just the West. It's the *Christian* West. "We cannot understand the West apart from the Christian faith, and we cannot understand the Christian faith as we live it today without understanding the history and culture of the West." Everything is "the"—*the* West, *the* Christian faith, *the* history and culture. "If future generations fail to learn to love our Western cultural heritage, we will lose it."[4]

He wants to teach us "to be men and women of the West"—but his examples are male and white—"we tell our children," he says, "about Odysseus, Achilles, and Aeneas, of Dante and Don Quixote, of Frodo and Gandalf."[5] What about Sappho, Hypatia, Hildegard, Julian, Mary Shelley, Guinevere, Joan of Arc, Kateri Tekakwitha, Harriet Tubman, Elizabeth Bennet, Sojourner Truth, Alice, Lucy Pevensie, Marie Curie, Princess Leia, Dorothy Day, Princess Eilonwy, Hermione Granger, Rosa Parks, Katniss Everdeen, even Wonder Woman?

So, Dreher's Benedict option is designed to shore up a construct, an artifact that is increasingly exposed as a monument to a European white male supremacy that has been inherited and turbocharged by Americans. Western culture is riddled with silences, myopias, distortions, biases both explicit and implicit, that are every day being unearthed, inspected, and classified through lenses of gender, class, and race. "Our Western cultural heritage" is not material for a textbook; the sources are imbalanced and cacophonous. And it matters who is *teaching about* that heritage.

Dreher seems to treat the Benedict option the way the third servant in Jesus's parable in Matthew 25 treats the one talent his master entrusts to him—hides it in the ground in order to protect it. The Benedictines I know handle what they receive the way the servants who got five and two talents do—they risk it on a whole variety of options. They have done this across the centuries.

The next two chapters will consider ways in which tradition emerges and works, in very different eras and contexts.

First is the early church, when monasticism, in a bewildering variety of forms, appeared on the Christian scene.

Second is the immediate aftermath of the Second Vatican Council, when American Benedictine women went on a journey that some of their contemporaries saw as falling off a cliff, but they themselves discovered was a walk along a Möbius strip. They ended up where they started—as Benedictines—but wholly reoriented. They learned in the marrow of their bones the truth in an aphorism of my teacher Jaroslav Pelikan: "Tradition is the living faith of the dead; traditionalism is the dead faith of the living."[6]

The people of Tevye's Anatevka weren't thinking about culture in a highly refined way, though they certainly respected the learning and insight of their rabbi. But in the course of *Fiddler on the Roof* they come to realize that their tradition is not uniform, that it doesn't answer all questions or solve all problems. They themselves are making their own positive revisionist contribution to it.

As a marvelous story in the Talmud has it, a group of rabbis overruled a decision by one of their number whose position had been certified on the spot by the voice of God. Subsequently, no less an authority than the prophet Elijah, when asked what God was doing while this debate was going on, replied, God "smiled and said: 'My children have triumphed over Me; My children have triumphed over Me.'"[7]

Tevye understands the vitality of tradition: "On the one hand, but on the other hand, but on the other hand . . . ."

chapter three

Long Ago[1]

I find it helpful, in understanding the past, to engage in time travel. I want to retroject a "modern person" into the ancient world, to see how some early Benedictine options play out in that scenario.

I turn to Katerina Ivanovna Marmeladov, in Dostoevsky's novel *Crime and Punishment*. She is evicted from her home on the very day of her husband's funeral. She exclaims in desperation, "There is justice and truth in the world, there is, I'll find it!" In a frenzy that is a prelude to madness she runs "shouting and weeping out into the street—with the vague purpose of finding justice somewhere, at once, immediately, and whatever the cost."[2] What she wants is for the world to make sense.

Discussions of justice too often lapse into the formal, the abstract; we too easily detach our language from the immediacy and tension of real life. The novelist—in Dostoevsky's case also, I warrant, a theologian of the first rank—reminds us that behind all theories of justice there are people *running at once, somewhere, to find it*, impelled by *a vague purpose*, but with a determined conviction that *there is justice and truth in the world, there is!*

Cynicism or Madness?

Dostoevsky's message is not reassuring or comfortable. Katerina Ivanovna's frantic search for justice does not succeed.

Such meager coherence as her world possesses disintegrates into insanity.

Another of Dostoevsky's characters, Ivan Fyodorovich Karamazov, presses the most haunting instance of injustice—the suffering of children—and suggests that in a world where God permits such things to happen the search for justice is bound to be futile. With a cynicism born of moral seriousness, Ivan declares he wants no part of such a world,[3] a world in which too much human life is, in the words of Thomas Hobbes I noted earlier, "solitary, poor, nasty, brutish, and short."[4]

The issue posed by Katerina Ivanovna and Ivan Fyodorovich—is cynicism the only alternative to madness in a world so manifestly unjust?—has been confronted and dealt with in many different ways in history, including the history of the church. Different understandings of injustice—of how to make sense of the world—have themselves been a source of theological discord.

There are four classic solutions to Ivan Karamazov's dilemma. Controversy over these solutions has exposed some of the most profound questions in Christian understanding of where and how the church is. It is significant that these four solutions were proposed either when "Christendom" had not yet come into being, or during the period of initial puzzling through what it meant for the church to be embraced by the world following the conversion of Emperor Constantine.

The "end of Christendom" in the twentieth century—a phenomenon that is not at all equivalent to the consequence of Rod Dreher's alleged "corrosive anti-Christian philosophy"[5]—is a fact of immense importance. We who live in Christendom's aftermath may have a good deal to learn from the experience of the church when Christendom was not yet, or was just beginning to be. Dreher certainly thinks so. But he and I extract different lessons.

Solution I:
Gnosticism—The Problem Is Entirely in God

The first of the classic solutions to Ivan's dilemma is Gnosticism. The church's struggle with Gnosticism in the second and third centuries was so bitter and protracted precisely because the Gnostics offered an attractive way of solving a theological problem. For the Gnostic, injustice is not a theological mystery, but the clue by which a theological mystery is solved.

Gnostics do not ask how God can permit injustice; rather, they conclude from the evidence around them that the world is not really the creation of the true God. "The world was not made by the primary God, but by a certain power far separated from him, and at a distance from that Authority who is supreme over the universe, and ignorant of the God who is above all."[6]

Whether a Gnostic considers the Creator to be benignly incompetent or viciously malevolent, the implication is the same: the world we inhabit is not our true home. We are prisoners here. Even the effort to promote justice is bound to fail because it is tangled in the web of the creator's limitations. To strive for justice would be to play a losing game, because the one who makes the rules is by nature unjust: "Marcion . . . declared him (who is proclaimed as God by the law and the prophets) to be the author of evils, a lover of war, inconstant in judgment, and contrary to himself."[7]

Marcion—who drank deeply at the Gnostic well, even if some scholars are hesitant to apply the term to him—turned the Bible upside down, making those who worked to establish justice in the earth—for example, Abel, Enoch, Noah, the patriarchs, all the prophets—into enemies of the true God, while Cain, the inhabitants of Sodom, the Egyptians, and "all the nations generally who walked in all sorts of abominations" were hailed as heralds and heirs of salvation.[8]

Why was Gnosticism so popular? It removed injustice from the category of problems for which human beings must take any responsibility. The world is out of joint because of a catastrophe in the divine realm. We obviously cannot do anything to correct a defect there.

What we are called to do is to make our escape. Thanks to the intrusion into the world of the true God's emissary, the Redeemer who appeared in Jesus—but was not truly incarnate, for that would have been to fall into the creator's trap—we have been blessed with the knowledge of our true home, our true origin, our true destiny. This knowledge springs us free.

Moreover, we learn that all of us—at least all of us who are children of the true God—are fundamentally the same, sparks of the divine, so we do not need to come to terms with the enormous variety of persons we meet in our day-to-day lives. Gnostic unity is the obliteration of all distinctions. Community is finally no problem because everyone who counts is exactly the same as everyone else who counts. The children of the true God are the ultimate homogeneous congregation.

To the true Gnostic, whose spirit has been awakened by the Redeemer, the injustice that so haunts the regular Christian believer is illusory. In one Gnostic text Jesus says: "Whoever has come to know the world has found a corpse. And whoever has found (this) corpse, of him the world is not worthy."[9] Another explains the apparent injustice of the crucifixion of Jesus as a trick: Simon of Cyrene, who carried the cross, was strung up on it while the Savior stood on the sidelines laughing.[10]

In Gnosticism, Katerina's bafflement and Ivan's anguish give way to laughter, for to one who really knows the truth, injustice is a joke—a rather clumsy joke at that, the sort of humor to be expected from a creator who could find nothing better than matter to work with. The Gnostic is the ancestor of anyone who says the gospel is exclusively about the spiritual life and should not be mixed up with politics and economics.

Solution II:
Pelagianism—The Problem Is Entirely in Us

If Gnosticism gives one classic answer to the problem of injustice—the source of injustice is exclusively in the divine realm—Pelagianism gives another classic answer: the source of injustice is exclusively in the human realm. The way to overcome injustice is to get our wills in line with God's will. We can do this.

The Pelagian is disturbed by social injustice, and would certainly never greet it with laughter as the Gnostic does. However, there is no sense that the problem is intractable, no torment of the sort we see in Ivan Karamazov, none of Katerina Marmeladov's perplexity. We simply have to pull ourselves together and will the good.

While God gets the ultimate credit for having made us so we are capable of doing what we should, "we have the power of accomplishing every good thing by action, speech, and thought."[11] If, for the Gnostic, justice and community are entirely incompatible because true unity with each other and with God belongs only to those who have risen above the world where justice itself is only a version of injustice; for the Pelagian, justice and community are entirely compatible because the human being is fully capable of willing, and hence doing, what God commands. When all will what God wills, justice is done and all are one.

Curiously, while Gnosticism is ultimately pessimistic about the world and Pelagianism ultimately optimistic, they share a strident individualism. The plight of other people just does not matter a great deal to the Gnostic or the Pelagian.

For the Gnostic, redemption is predestined, so there is not much point worrying about the fate of others—those who are not saved could not be saved anyway.

For the Pelagian, redemption is entirely in our own power, so there is not much point worrying about the fate of others—those who are not saved did not want to be saved anyway.

And just as Gnosticism and Pelagianism exalt individualism, so do they both discount individuality.

As we saw already, all Gnostics are ultimately sparks of the same divine substance, indistinguishable from one another. For the Pelagian, our wills are not finally our own, but are indistinguishable from the single will of God.

For the Gnostic, true justice and true community can coalesce only in a realm entirely divorced from the world—Katerina Ivanovna, by running into the street instead of flying up into the highest heaven, was looking for justice in the wrong place. For the Pelagian, true justice and true community can coalesce fully in this world if we just try hard enough—Katerina Ivanovna, going with "a vague intention" of finding justice, was not sufficiently determined.

"Pure" Gnostics and "pure" Pelagians were probably as rare in the early church as they are today, but the terms designate tendencies that can be found in Christian attitudes in every age.

Each of the two positions in its own way dismisses from the Christian agenda the murky, chaotic, baffling, painful, challenging realm of social life. I do not have to figure out how to live in some sort of harmony with all sorts and conditions of people. If am a Gnostic, those who are different from me are hopelessly inferior to me. If I am a Pelagian, those who are different from me only appear to be different.

Solution III: Donatism—Church versus World

The patristic period offers two paradigms of the church that mediate between the Gnostic and the Pelagian.

Much of the struggle today over the proper role of the church in issues of justice can be seen as the playing out of a debate implied in two fourth-century developments that constitute solutions three and four to Katerina Ivanovna and Ivan Fyodorovich's dilemma: Donatism and monasticism.

Prior to Constantine's conversion the church had been a victim of injustice. Tertullian's epigram, "the blood of Christians is seed,"[12] underscores the fact that injustice suffered is often a powerful bonding force for unity.

With Constantine, the schemes of survival the church had developed through ten generations since the time of the apostles suddenly became irrelevant. Within a very brief time new proposals were made for preserving some of the old ideals within a radically altered context.

The Donatists take a Pelagian view of themselves and a Gnostic view of everyone else. The church becomes a fortress of justice and unity in the midst of a world unjust and chaotic. The church must keep itself unspotted.

If anyone, especially a bishop, did anything remiss during the recent persecution, the Donatists say, that person's treason spreads like an infection through the church. We must avoid contact with anyone who is linked, by however tenuous a chain of influences, with anyone who has in any way fallen short of unadulterated purity in doctrine and practice.

The ideal of a church totally different from "the world" is highly appealing to anyone who is eager for a safe haven, but Saint Augustine was quick to point out that the church is hardly so isolated. One who enters the church, he says, "is bound to see drunkards, misers, tricksters, gamblers, adulterers, fornicators, people wearing amulets, assiduous clients of sorcerers, astrologers. . . . The same crowds that press into the churches on Christian festivals also fill the theatres on pagan holidays."[13]

To the Donatist, the portrait of the church painted by Augustine is grotesque, a chamber of horrors, and shows Augustine insufficiently repulsed by the world outside the church, dangerously unaware that compromise is a greater threat to the church than persecution had ever been. Concern for injustice in the world outside the church paled into insignificance when contrasted with the desperate need to preserve purity within. The questions posed by Katerina Ivanovna and Ivan Fyodorovich would be drowned out by the noise of the controversy stirred up by the Donatists.

"Pure" Donatists, like "pure" Gnostics and "pure" Pelagians, are rare, but the Donastist spirit is not hard to find in the churches today or at any time. The church is not for the sake of a world that is hurting. Rather, it is a refuge from a world that is hazardous. The image that comes to mind is not so much a sheepfold with a gate as a castle with a drawbridge, and the drawbridge pulled up.

Solution IV:
Monasticism—"A School for the Lord's Service"

In Donatism, we see Christians reacting to their new social and political status by turning inward and shutting out the world that now too eagerly wants to embrace the church. In monasticism, we see the church turning outward to embrace the world.

On first hearing, this claim sounds outlandish. The men and women who, in the fourth century, flocked by the tens of thousands to colonize the desert appear to be almost classically Donatist: separate from the world.

The monks went into the desert not to maintain their purity, however, but to do unremitting battle with the demons: the "world" that needed to be overcome was more sharply confronted in the cell than in the countless distractions of daily life in society. The monastery was most certainly not an escape or haven.

The world-embracing monastic spirit soon came to full expression in the establishment created by Saint Basil of Caesarea, who in the mid-fourth century fashioned the most efficient social welfare institution the Roman world had ever known, and then, two centuries later, in the Rule of Saint Benedict, which grounds justice in repentance, unity in hospitality, and renewal in discipline.

Monastic history is far from being uniform or simple. There have been monks who would qualify spiritually as Gnostics or Pelagians or Donatists. But the fundamental, characteristic monastic instinct is different from these.

The Gnostic is cynical about the world, the Pelagian is romantic, and the Donatist belligerent. The monk or sister views the world ironically, acknowledging the world, including the human self, as God's good creation that has gone awry, and seeing himself or herself as able, with the help of others, and always wary of our limitless capacity to fool ourselves, to participate in the rebuilding of both world and self.

The genius of monasticism is its refusal to propose a neat, no-loose-ends answer to the puzzle of injustice and community in the church and the world. The Gnostics said the problem is in God, the Pelagians located the problem in us, the Donatists set the church as the complete answer over against the world as the total problem. Benedict's Rule avoids all such sharp lines of demarcation. Monks do not write off the world as a lost cause.

The monastery is not a fortress, but "a school for the Lord's service" (Prol. 45). The Rule itself does not map the whole spiritual universe, but is "this little rule that we have written for beginners" (73.8). Growth is a governing metaphor of Benedictine spirituality. Every feast day of Benedict monks and sisters who have spent fifty or sixty years in the order renew their pledge to seek God.

Benedictines make no claim to having solved conclusively Katerina Ivanova and Ivan Fyodorovich's dilemma, but they do know that an adequate answer cannot be framed abstractly, in detachment. They know that you do not wait to live the Christian life until you have decided what it is. The God who demands justice can be found only through a disciplined life of repentance and hospitality.

Justice and Hospitality

It is sad beyond measure that when Katerina Ivanovna rushes into the street she does not find her way to a monastery. What she really seeks is not justice, but hospitality. The demand for justice would require her to plead her case. She is in no condition to do that. Moreover, in strictly legal terms her case could probably be pulverized by a clever lawyer on the other side.

No, what she requires is to be taken in and given rest, no questions asked. "First of all, (the monks and the guest) are to pray together and thus be united in peace" (53.4). The guest is to be received as Christ, and "great care and concern are to be shown in receiving poor people and pilgrims, because in them more particularly Christ is received" (53.1, 7, 15).

Indeed, Benedict's Rule assigns only three persons the place of Christ in the monastery: the abbot, the guest, and the invalid (2.2; 53.1; 36.1-2).

Had Katerina Ivanovna come to a monastery, she would not have had to justify herself. She would simply have been received as though she were Christ. If she had tried to "explain" her case to the monks, she would have been as gently comical as the Prodigal Son, who speaks his well-rehearsed line—"Father, I have sinned against heaven and before you; I am no longer worthy to be called your son" (Luke 15:21)—while his father is showering him with welcoming embraces and kisses. He looks for justice—"Treat me as one of your hired servants"—and gets a party.

Hospitality and Advocacy

Hospitality by itself is not enough. The church is not big enough to receive everybody. Not everybody who is hurting wants to come into the church. Moreover, hospitality if divorced entirely from advocacy can foster an unhealthy dependence. In our own time monks and sisters are following their vocation beyond hospitality into frontline, public involvement in matters of social justice—poverty, war, discrimination. They do so in the spirit of renewal fostered by the ancient cry, *"Ad fontes!"*— "To the sources!"

Following the mandate from Vatican II, as monks and sisters have looked again at the documents on which their institutions are founded, they have discovered a strong impetus for engagement with the world. The titles they give their statements of purpose are revealing: *Renew and Create,* and *Call to Life.* The title of a book that will get extensive attention in chapter 4, about the renewal process among American Benedictine women, is especially graphic: *Climb Along the Cutting Edge.*[14]

The direct engagement of monks and sisters with the world is a leading fact of contemporary church history. As has often been true in the past, what the monks and sisters are doing causes a good deal of consternation among bishops and other administrators. But the activists claim, with good cause, that what they are doing is not a deviation from the original monastic charism but is a retrieval of that charism and a valid expression of it in our time.

The effectiveness of monks and sisters in the work for justice can be traced to the authenticity of their witness—it is simply evident that prior to their advocacy is their hospitality; they accept without checking credentials those whose fight for justice they are supporting and even joining.

Hospitality and Community

Hospitality links justice and community, or rather, it puts them in proper perspective.

The trouble with justice and community as we usually understand them is that those in power define the terms. Katerina Ivanovna is outside the ranks of those who determine what counts as justice. It is usually the outcasts who are condemned for threatening community. Those who call the churches to account for their complicity in white supremacy are denounced for being "divisive," for "mixing up the church with politics." Churches that ordain women, not those that refuse to do so, are accused of dashing hopes for church unity. Jesus's association with sinners, not the prior exclusion of those persons from religious and civil society, was called a scandal.

If Benedict sets forth in classical form the theological rationale for hospitality, Basil had already given practical expression to the ideal—and Basil is cited by Benedict as worthy of special attention (73.5). Here is what Basil's friend, Gregory of Nazianzus, says about Basil's care for those most wretched of ancient outcasts, the lepers, who previously "were driven away from their cities and homes and public places and fountains, . . . and from their own dearest ones. . . . He did not therefore disdain to honor with his lips this disease, . . . but saluted them as brethren. . . . Others have had their cooks, and splendid tables, and the devices and dainties of confectioners, and exquisite carriages, and soft, flowing robes; Basil's care was for the sick, and the relief of their wounds, and the imitation of Christ, by cleansing leprosy, not by a word, but in deed."[15]

Basil's care for those in need was characteristic of Christians more generally. Emperor Julian, passionately committed to the restoration of the ancient Greek religion, chides his priests for letting the Christians so spectacularly outdo them in charity—"the impious Galileans support not only their own poor but ours as well."[16]

Julian was bitter enough against Christianity to begrudge the church any compliment. His reference to hospitality and advocacy for "the world" outside the bounds of the church, a ministry that was quickly becoming a hallmark of monasticism, is the most valuable sort of evidence of the early church's actual commitment to justice, and of the effect of that action for justice in creating community across divisions—"not only their own poor but ours as well."

Christian Existence Is Social by Nature

If Benedict makes clear that hospitality is of the essence of the church's life, not a luxury to be afforded only when the house is in order, Basil makes a corresponding claim for the fundamentally social character of Christian existence.

- "None of us is self-sufficient even as regards bodily needs,
  . . . so in the solitary life both what we have becomes use-
  less and what we lack becomes unprocurable, since God
  the Creator ordained that we need one another."

- Living separately, one "will not even recognize his/[her]
  defects readily, not having anyone to reprove him/her or
  set him/her right with kindness and compassion."

- There are many divine commandments, and a group can
  perform them, while an individual, by doing one com-
  mandment, is hindered from another, "for example, when
  we visit a sick [person] we cannot receive a stranger; when
  we bestow and distribute the necessaries of life—especially when these ministrations have to be performed at
  a distance—we neglect work; so that the greatest com-
  mandment of all and that which conduces to salvation is
  neglected, and neither is the hungry fed nor the naked
  clothed."[17]

Basil has understood that Christian virtues are by their nature communal. He sees the practical implications of Paul's
image of the church as a body—what one member does is as if
done by the other members as well. This is of cardinal importance for the church's involvement in issues of justice: those
Christians who are directly involved are acting on behalf of all
Christians.

The parable of the Good Samaritan makes the double point.
The Samaritan treats the victim as his neighbor, but Jesus asks
the rich young man, "[Who] was a neighbor to the man who
fell into the hands of the robbers?" (Luke 10:36). In other words,
just as we must be hospitable to those who need help, so must
we be hospitable to those among us who provide that help, even
if we have reservations about the credentials either of those
ministering or of those being ministered to.

Gregory of Nazianzus is urging Christians to imitate Basil in his welcoming of lepers, and not to reject Basil because of his association with those whose uncleanness endangers good order in the society. Katerina Ivanovna's husband was a scoundrel, her daughter is a prostitute, she herself something of a scatterbrain. To become her advocate would certainly not do any good for the reputation of the church among the social, intellectual, and political elite. To suggest that "of such is the kingdom of heaven" would scandalize good church people.

Justice and Repentance

What Jesus told the Pharisees is what Augustine told the Donatists, and Martin Luther King Jr. told the white pastors of Birmingham, Alabama: all, including "good church people," are sinners, and self-righteousness is a more virulent source of division than is the prophetic call for justice. "It is unfortunate that demonstrations are taking place in Birmingham," wrote King from jail, "but it is even more unfortunate that the city's white power structure left the Negro community with no alternative."[18]

King denies that he and his followers are "the creators of tension: We merely bring to the surface the hidden tension that is already alive."[19] "The question is not whether we will be extremists, but what kind of extremists we will be. . . . Will we be extremists for the preservation of injustice or for the extension of justice?"[20]

Repentance is not a once-and-for-all cleansing, but a daily discipline, especially for those who think they do not need it, whether because they are Gnostics who are above the world, or Pelagians who have figured out the world, or Donatists who have gone to the barricades against the world.

Repentance is also necessary for those who are committed to justice. It is terribly easy for those whose cause is just to blur the line between what they are working for and their own reputation and glory. As King notes: "Mindful of the difficulties involved, we decided to undertake a process of self-purification."[21] But then action must be taken: "We will have to repent in this generation not merely for the hateful words and actions of the bad people but for the appalling silence of the good people."[22] "I have watched white churchmen stand on the sideline and mouth pious irrelevancies and sanctimonious trivialities. In the midst of a mighty struggle to rid our nation of racial and economic injustice, I have heard many ministers say: 'Those are social issues, with which the gospel has no real concern.' And I have watched many churches commit themselves to a completely otherworldly religion which makes a strange, un-biblical distinction between body and soul, between the sacred and the secular."[23]

Repentance is fundamental to any Christian spirituality that would link justice and community, for without repentance, work for justice slips into a kind of ideological dogmatism. Alexander Solzhenitsyn has sketched the modem problem sharply: "The gift of repentance, which perhaps more than anything else distinguishes (human beings) from the animal world, is particularly difficult for modern (persons) to recover. We have, every last one of us, grown ashamed of this feeling; and its effect on social life anywhere on earth is less and less easy to discern. The habit of repentance is lost to our whole callous and chaotic age."[24]

After summing up the threats to our planet, Solzhenitsyn concludes: "We can say without suspicion of overstatement that without repentance it is in any case doubtful if we can survive."[25]

Repentance is necessary not only because without it we can perpetrate injustice while fighting for justice, but also because without it we can soon lose heart. The reason monks and sisters stick with the work for justice after many others have left the field for other, more immediately gratifying, enterprises is the monastic awareness that things take time, the conviction that an effort begun in a previous generation will be carried on by generations yet to come.

Yet patience does not breed complacency; knowing that "things take time" is no excuse for telling victims of injustice to "wait" to press their case, as one white Christian wrote to King: "It is possible that you are in too great a religious hurry. It has taken Christianity almost two thousand years to accomplish what it has. The teachings of Christ take time to come to earth."[26]

Renewal and Discipline

In the monastic tradition, repentance fuses with humility to create an engine for social change, a "spirituality for the long haul," to use the title of a book by the noted ecumenist and pioneer of ecumenical study, Robert Bilheimer.[27]

Without repentance, without a spirituality for the long haul of a sort exemplified by monastic ideals and practice, the church's involvement in issues of justice will not be distinguishable from ideology. While there may be, as a result of church involvement, a momentary advance toward justice, there will probably not be much sustained or sustainable rebuilding of human community. In Solzhenitsyn's terms, part of the mission of the church is to show the human community how to repent, how to relearn a habit that "is lost to our whole callous and chaotic age."

We learn habits, or relearn them, by practice. Today in America people are little willing to work at things for very long. Instant gratification is sought and expected. If the wished-for result—whether a fancy new car or a bigger church budget and expanding membership roll—is not forthcoming, some new gimmick will be tried for a while. It is here that monasticism may have its most important message for today's church.

Saint Anthony, the first Christian monk, started out at age eighteen on a discipline of life that would last eighty-seven years (he died at one hundred and five). Of course he did not know at the start how long a race he had to run, but Saint Athanasius, in his *Life of Anthony*, suggests that one of the most powerful arguments the devil used to try to dissuade Anthony from his commitment was the simple reminder of "the length of the time."[28]

Benedict, reflecting on two centuries of accumulated monastic experience and theory, concludes his long chapter on the steps of humility with a declaration about the results of discipline: "All that the monk once performed with dread, he will now begin to observe without effort, as though naturally, from habit, no longer out of fear of hell, but out of love for Christ, good habit and delight in virtue" (7.68-69).

Monks and sisters know that some things are worth doing, and continuing to do, even if you don't particularly like them— that pearls of great price are not only pearls, but also of great price. When we recognize that genuine rebuilding—of ourselves, our churches, our communities—requires discipline, we pray for it as Augustine prayed for chastity[29]: "Lord, give it to us—but not yet."

Options

Benedict provides an alternative to the Gnostic, the Pelagian, and the Donatist solutions to what ails us. It seems to me that Rod Dreher has stirred Pelagian and Donatist prescriptions into the mix of the Benedict option. With Pelagius, he talks about aligning our wills and the will of God in a manner that makes it more straightforward than I think it is. With the Donatists, he calls for a "pure" church—especially in the gathering of neighborhoods of the like-minded and in the total withdrawal from public schools (features of *the* Option that will figure prominently in Part Four). I detect even a trace of Gnosticism in Dreher's "world growing cold, dead, and dark."

Benedictine options that I see already in the early centuries— hospitality, repentance, discipline, persistence—are certainly saluted by Dreher, but he encompasses them all in an initial retreat from the world. Benedict, instructed by his great predecessor, Basil, establishes the relationship with the world first, and develops those options in ongoing involvement with the world. Options aren't something that the monks perfect and then offer to the larger society. It is only in the interaction that options come to life—and God is operating on both sides of the collaboration.

Benedictine options make clear that Katerina Ivanovna Marmeladov's madness is not inevitable, and that Ivan Fyodorovich Karamazov's cynicism is not the only honest conclusion.

chapter four

A Wagonload of Trouble[1]

There are very few things I claim to know for sure. One of them is this: feminism is for the sake of everyone, not just women. I've published brief accounts of a couple of feminist conversion experiences I've had.[2] There was a degree of pain while they were in progress. Nothing, though, could persuade me to return to the pre-conversion days when guys like me were the standard against which "the human" was assessed. I know what John Newton meant in "Amazing Grace": "I was blind but now I see."

I envy women the experience many of them have had, in the words of my friend, theologian Mary Bednarowski, of living in and through recent "wild and wonderful" years.[3] I am enormously grateful for what their experience, and their wide-ranging and deep-probing reflections on that experience, have taught me, how they have stripped the veil from my eyes.

Yet I can't know firsthand the exhilaration of "every discourse hurling itself against impossibility";[4] of what it's like to be "resident aliens and intimate outsiders";[5] of coming to hear one's own silence and experience one's own invisibility; to discover a camaraderie with others whom you don't have to explain yourself to.

Early in my career I attended a feminist theology conference. There were two hundred women in the room, five men. We five laughed at all the wrong places. We didn't get it when everyone else laughed. Years later I was recounting this story. A woman within earshot said, "Oh, I was at that meeting. I had just started teaching in an otherwise all-male department. I remember going home that evening and saying to my husband, 'For the first time in months I knew where to laugh!'"

So many things are called "revolutionary" these days that a genuine revolution may slip by almost undetected. So many things are in flux these days that a genuine revolution, if detected, may be mistaken for anarchy.

In 1977 a book about a revolution was published, a revolution that many people at the time did not know about, and that was misinterpreted, by some who did know about it, as an unprincipled jettisoning of traditions by women who had lost all sense of who they are and where they belong. The authors wanted future generations to know what happened, and their own contemporaries to know how to interpret the revolution correctly.

1977 was long ago—though in the Benedictine timeframe of a millennium and a half, just the blink of an eye. The story that Joan Chittister, OSB, Stephanie Campbell, OSB, Mary Collins, OSB, Ernestine Johann, OSB, and Johnette Putnam, OSB, tell in *Climb Along the Cutting Edge: An Analysis of Change in Religious Life* provides an intense and currently relevant insight into Benedictine options.

"Now the Sisters Are Coming"

The way was prepared in 1852 for the recognition that Benedictine women offered at least an alternative, and more likely several, to a single Benedict option.

On June 12 that year, three Benedictine sisters left their community at Eichstätt in Bavaria. Sailing from Bremen, they landed in New York on July 3. Prior Boniface Wimmer, OSB, who had invited them to come to America, failed to meet them or have anyone else do so, but the sisters made their way, over four days, to Saint Vincent Archabbey in Latrobe, Pennsylvania. The story goes that "when the wagon carrying the sisters and their luggage neared the monastery on July 8, 1852, a lay brother working in the fields ran to report to Prior Boniface that 'a wagonload of trouble' was coming up the hill."[6]

Five years later, shortly after Wimmer had established Saint John's Abbey in Minnesota, there was another moment perceived as "trouble." Fr. Alexius Roetzer, one of the original group of monks at Saint John's, wrote to (now) Abbot Boniface: "As soon as one trouble is over another shows up. Now the sisters are coming."[7]

Climb Along the Cutting Edge is a study of attitudes and actions of members of the Federation of Saint Scholastica, one of four groups of American Benedictine sisters, who participated during the decade 1966–75 in a series of meetings to consider Vatican II's mandate in *Perfectae Caritatis*, the Decree on the Adaptation and Renewal of Religious Life.[8] It's a story of a wagonload of trouble—but, in terms made famous by the late civil rights hero, John Lewis, "good trouble." Or, as Wimmer wrote in 1859 to his benefactor, King Ludwig of Bavaria, "It is always difficult to find good superiors, even for monasteries, and an audacious energetic woman, if she does not possess the discretion becoming to the female sex, can cause more inconvenience than an unruly man."[9]

Climb Along the Cutting Edge draws upon many sources, but primarily upon a comprehensive and scientifically designed survey of nearly two hundred sisters who had participated in the revolution over a period of a decade.

Delegates to the "Renewal Chapters," as the meetings were called, were not a cross-section of the membership. There were among them many prioresses and other administrators, and the average educational level was high. But they ranged widely in age, and one of the more interesting conclusions of the book is the finding that the revolution cannot be attributed to the young sisters. The degree of zeal for change and acceptance of change simply did not correlate with age.

The limitation of the study to a group within the Federation is one of its strengths. There is no detailed information about the impact of change on this or that individual monastery. Some of the statistics from the survey give clear hints that the twenty-three monasteries of the Federation are not by any means cast in the same mold. There would be as many different stories of change as there were monasteries.

There is next to nothing about the responses of those who thought the changes either too little too late or too much too soon. Those were stories worth telling, but they are not this story. They would divert attention from the point this story is trying to make.

Those who undertook this project began with a desire to learn what the revolutionaries perceived had happened. On the basis of knowledge gathered in the survey, the investigators concluded that the revolution worked because it was perceived by those intimately involved in it to be a genuine renewal—a rebuilding, if you will—not at all a restoration.

The delegates to the Renewal Chapters believed they were still Benedictines; believed, in fact, that they were better Benedictines than they were before. The investigators make the additional judgment that the perception of continuity, of the reality of renewal, was in fact accurate.

The book, then, is partisan, but in a special sense—in a sense that makes it a genuine work of history as well as an historical document. The revolutionaries who wrote the book are partisans of the middle.

Hundreds of their colleagues were revolutionaries of the extreme and rode the wave of revolution right out of the boundaries within which the revolution was happening. Very few people knew anything about women religious, but nearly everybody knew that sisters were leaving the orders in great numbers. The "crisis" of monastic and priestly life attracted publicity. The extreme response, as always, made the best press copy.

But what of those who were no less revolutionary, and yet, when the crisis subsided, found themselves still in the order?

Sisters Joan, Stephanie, Mary, Ernestine, and Johnette knew in their own experience the full force of the question, "Why, after all, stick with it?" They stuck with it. Their book offers at least a partial explanation.

One of the central puzzles to which the book addresses itself is the ability of so many women to alter virtually every aspect of their behavior while maintaining a sense of continuity with the past. How did it come about that they could ask one another, half incredulously, "Did we *really* do those things back then?" and still affirm that who they were then is not radically discontinuous with who they are now?

Historical Identity

American Benedictine sisters are of course not alone in experiencing a trauma of historical identity.

Pope Saint John XXIII's bold confidence that the Holy Spirit would blow through the church's windows if they were opened has, at the very least, given the Spirit ample opportunity to gust this way and that. The Catholic Church got stirred up as it had not been for nearly five centuries. The documents of Vatican II, despite the occasional paragraph that tries to shut a window the previous paragraph has just shoved open, provide strong impetus for change—even more important, for *thinking about* change—in virtually every aspect of the church's life.

Some of the documents use many words to say a few things. *Perfectae Caritatis*, which looms large in *Climb Along the Cutting Edge*, uses a few words to say what turned out to be many things.

Among the norms for renewal are adherence to the gospel, acceptance and retention of the spirit and aims of each institute's founder, and the making of wise judgments about the contemporary world in the light of faith. Chittister et al. tell what happens when those norms are taken seriously—when, in a delicious irony, twenty-five hundred men sitting in Rome wrote a charter for revolution for a group of American women.

There is a partial explanation for the irony, however. By the mid-1970s the church as a whole was in ferment—or chaos, as some called it—but the trauma of historical identity was pecu-liarly acute for American Benedictine sisters because for their entire history of more than a hundred years the church's officials and its legal system had failed quite completely to comprehend the nature of their life. With example after example, the book makes clear the incongruity of the imposition of strict enclosure on the life of American Benedictine sisters, who from the time they arrived in this country were actively engaged in parochial work, primarily teaching.

Enclosure was at odds with the experience and requirements of the apostolic work to which the American Benedictine sisters were committed, but enclosure was sanctioned by a theological principle.

According to this theological tenet, women and men religious served the church by providing living examples of rejection of the profane in favor of the sacred—in a way, a testimony to Dreher's version of the Benedict option. As I noted in chapter 1, there is an ancient tradition of thinking about the monastic life as the "angelic" life, in consequence of which the monastery should not be tainted by "the world."

But the theological principle was not applied evenhandedly.

Strict enclosure was never imposed on men religious. Women were thought to be weaker, more susceptible to temptation, hence more in need of being fenced off from the outside world.

The regulation of women religious is a particularly vivid il-lustration of sexism in the church. One of the most stirring themes in *Climb Along the Cutting Edge* is the sisters' overcom-ing deeply ingrained patterns of dependence on and deference to male authority. The declaration of a large majority of the sisters surveyed, that they consider themselves competent to make decisions about the religious life for themselves, is perhaps the single most dramatic indicator of the "good trouble" that sparked the revolution.

The requirement of enclosure led to countless anomalies: for instance, would the schoolteacher, after a meeting with parents, join them in refreshments, or leave because she was not supposed to eat with secular persons? In such ways the sisters experienced inner conflicts of role-definition and hence of self-definition.

But the anomalies of enclosure went even deeper—into the creation and maintenance of an "enclosure mentality" that worked against the development of a genuine community within the enclosure.

Just as sisters were supposed to avoid contact with outsiders, so they were to be wary of attachments to insiders. Life within the enclosure was so organized that real community was hard to nurture. Even recreation was required of everyone in the same room at the same time.

There was little opportunity for the solitude upon which true companionship depends. There was fear of particular friendships, which are in fact a necessary basis of friendship for the whole community. Sisters became specialists in love of God, as if Jesus had not yoked love for God inextricably to love for neighbor.

This problem had deep roots. A careful study of medieval monasticism demonstrates that "the full expression of the view that close friendship is not only congruent with true community, but even constitutive of it, appeared only in the twelfth century, *and did not long survive.*"[10]

This "specialness" of the sisters was expressed most directly in their liturgical life, technically defined as "choral prayer." The gathering of the entire community several times a day for prayer has been a feature of Benedictine monastic life from the beginning, but time and again reformers have arisen to remind Benedictines that even if choral prayer is a distinguishing feature of their life, it is nevertheless only one feature among many.

The elaboration of liturgy, so that it pushes nearly every other activity off the schedule, has been a recurrent temptation in Benedictine history. The recent reduction of services, both in number and in length, among the Benedictine sisters appears to many outside, and even to some within the order, to be a radical rejection of Benedictine tradition.

As even slight acquaintance with church history shows, however, the recent revisions are not without precedent. As Chittister et al. make clear, and as I noted in chapter 1, Benedict himself gave the charter for altering the pattern of monastic liturgical life. He set down a detailed schedule, then added that anyone who could think of something better was free to make changes.

All is not arbitrary, however. To eliminate choral prayer—the activity to which Benedict gave the name *opus Dei*, "work of God"—would be to give up legitimate claim to the Benedictine heritage. To have two or three services a day instead of seven, though, does not in any way imperil the inheritance.

The reason the revolution among American Benedictine sisters appears anarchic to some observers is that the sense of history with which most Americans and most Catholics function is far too restricted. The life of pre-Vatican II Benedictine sisters was so different from the life of other Christian women that it was assumed the patterns must have been very ancient. The practical meaning of "medieval" for many people would have been "contemporary monastic life."

But the past is a great expanse, itself a scene of constant change. One result of Vatican II's mandate to each institute to recover the aims and spirit of its founder was the discovery by the Benedictine sisters that their life was being lived not according to the spirit of Saint Benedict, but according to the forms of eighteenth- and nineteenth-century German cultural monastic practice as codified by the 1918 Code of Canon Law.

It turned out that the directive in *Perfectae Caritatis* to accept and retain the spirit and aims of each institute's founder was more radical than the directive to make wise judgments about the contemporary world. Dreher talks about restoration of *the* tradition. Benedictine sisters were liberated when they discovered how various the *traditions* are.

Learning To Do Their Own Work

What was thought to be "traditional" was itself an aberration within the tradition. A shortsighted, static view of history had to be overcome by a comprehensive, dynamic view of history. It was not easy for such research and rethinking to happen among the sisters. They had been enclosed not only from the secular world at large but also from the scholarly world.

To be sure, there were many college degrees to their credit—advanced degrees too—but nearly all the training had in view the practical application to the apostolates, primarily teaching in and administering parochial schools. Until the 1950s, advanced theological education for Benedictine sisters was unheard of.

It was through pioneering work at Saint Benedict's Monastery in Minnesota, and then at neighboring Saint John's Abbey, that sisters began to have opened to them the possibility for rigorous training in theology, both dogmatic and historical. The sisters during the revolution learned quickly how to do their own historical and doctrinal work.

At the beginning of the renewal decade they called in expert counselors, as they had always done in the past. By the end of the decade they were expressing gratitude for the help advisers had given them—and no longer inviting them to meetings. The sisters were able to chart their own course through a decade of revolution.

When the decade began, there was much apprehensiveness, because the very process of questioning, considering options, speaking boldly was new. Whether a sister had been professed for five years or for fifty, her life and attitudes and habits had been shaped by a clear concept of obedience and penance. The regimen was designed to suppress individual initiative and spontaneity, as though they were necessarily in conflict with humility.

A more humane and faithful understanding of Benedict's notion of humility—that it consists primarily in monastics' clear and honest assessment of their own spiritual strengths and weaknesses and their consequent acceptance of who they are—was current among Benedictine men, but had had virtually no impact on Benedictine women, or on Catholic men who had the power and authority to decide how Benedictine women should live.

Dreher writes that in the 1960s "the freedom of the individual to fulfill his own desires became our cultural lodestar, and the rapid falling away of American morality from its Christian ideal began as a result. Despite a conservative backlash in the 1980s, Psychological Man won decisively and now owns the culture—including most churches—as surely as the Ostrogoths, Visigoths, Vandals, and other conquering peoples owned the remains of the Western Roman Empire."[11]

Elsewhere, Dreher says that "in the end, either Christ is the center of our lives, or the Self and all its idolatries are." And the next sentence is one I quoted in the introduction to Part One: "There is no middle ground."[12]

Dreher sneers at "Psychological Man" and "the Self." But the Benedictine sisters demonstrate how critical the self is to a real humility—how it was crucial for women (not just monastic women) to provide their own positive alternative to Psychological Man, namely, Psychological Woman. On this point, as much as any, my assessment of current culture is diametrically opposed to Dreher's. Psychology has not "replaced" religion, as he says Freud tried to do.[13] It has come to religion's aid.

Climb Along the Cutting Edge tells of the surprise, even exhilaration, experienced by the sisters as they came to recognize strengths and competencies in one another and in themselves, and developed confidence to take risks. They began to suspect that obedience could be, as Benedict had intended, an open door on freedom, not one shut in its face. But they could not know where all this would lead them.

Revolution meant a new and unspecified kind of future—for which the sisters were giving up the satisfaction and security of the knowledge that "What I am doing now I will also be doing on the day I die."

At the time of writing their book the sisters were in a future they could at best have dimly foreseen a decade earlier. From the perspective of their new now, the way things had been had a dreamlike quality. In that earlier time, their life in their new now would have seemed a tale of fantasy. Very likely they would have been repelled by a vision of their new life; from the pre-Vatican II perspective, the way they were living now would have appeared almost indistinguishable from the life they had renounced in order to become religious in the first place.

However restive an individual sister might have felt under the pre-Vatican II system, she would characteristically have interpreted her restiveness as a sign of the distance she had yet to go in her pursuit of religious perfection. It would not have occurred to her that her uneasiness might be a protest from the depths of her Benedictine commitment against the outward manifestations of that commitment.

Memories of the Process of Change

In the course of a decade, many women came to the conviction that a style of life radically different from what they had known was in fact a more adequate expression of the principles that had originally inspired them to make lifetime vows. *Climb Along the Cutting Edge* represents an attempt by some of them to record and analyze the memories of the process of change—before the memories were further colored by subsequent developments and further eroded simply by the passage of time.

The book does not begin with the question: "Are we Benedictines?" Rather, it states the hypothesis: "We are Benedictines," then sets out to prove it. The book concludes, then, not with a "yes" or a "no," but with a QED.

Though each chapter of *Climb Along the Cutting Edge* is the work of an individual sister, it reflects repeated discussion and critique in daily meetings of the entire group over a period of several weeks.

The first chapter depends only marginally on the survey. Its author attempts to give an impression of the life of American Benedictine sisters before and after the revolution.

Any such attempt is bound to have a touch of caricature, but the sharp lines in which the life prior to Vatican II is sketched are perhaps a necessary corrective to a popular view of the life of women religious, shaped by such cultural phenomena as the motion picture "Lilies of the Field," the television serial "The Flying Nun," and the novel, subsequently adapted for television, *In This House of Brede*. It would be foolish to deny that the values of charity and self-denial and humor portrayed there so attractively were illusory, or inappropriate to the monastic tradition.

But it is important that such romantic views of the life of women religious be balanced against a realistic assessment of the spiritual liabilities of that pattern of life.

The second chapter explores the theological dimension of the revolution.

Vatican II put the church itself at the head of the agenda for theological reflection. It quickly became clear to the American Benedictine sisters that the fundamental definition of the church as "the people of God" had profound implications for their understanding of their own role within that "people." Writing a quarter-century later, a group of Benedictine sisters underscored the importance of this tectonic shift: "As soon as this [hierarchical] pyramid-image collapsed into the circle-image, authority found its rightful place within the circle of the People of God at the service of God and the community."[14] Holiness came to be seen not as a commodity of which the sister had purchased a bundle by her renunciations, but as a gift of the Spirit that is not limited to persons of a particular status in the church.

Spirituality was seen to be directly dependent on the vitality and dynamism of community life; it could no longer be a private affair between the sister and her heavenly spouse, Christ. The entire church was being challenged by a new understanding of the liturgy as a community action, not as a priestly act for viewing and veneration. Such a change was bound to influence sisters' theological self-understanding, since frequent participation in the Eucharist was integral to their life as Benedictines.

In short, the sisters could have remained content as they were only if the theology of the church did not apply to them.

The third chapter describes what happens when people get down to basics. As preparations for the first Renewal Chapter were being made and committees were appointed to prepare position papers on various questions that were sure to be disputed, two of the monasteries requested that Benedictinism itself be a subject of inquiry.

The request was at first rejected. The proposers persisted, and the topic was adopted as one of serious study. From the research and reflection done on the Rule of Benedict in the context of the two hundred years of monastic development prior to its writing, and on the history of the Benedictine tradition itself, came the growing awareness that the distant past could—must—correct a present that had been determined by a quite recent past. The sisters' "discovery" of the resources for renewal in their basic charter demonstrates how the Rule deserves its reputation for "discretion."

The fourth chapter deals with what everyone who has ever functioned within an organization knows, whether religious, political, business, or academic: procedure and substance cannot be disentangled. The way you do something has a profound effect on the thing you are doing.

Vatican II gave some guidelines for renewal of religious institutes—in particular, deliberations were to take place in chapters, that is, meetings with wide representation. Each institute, however, had its own customs. Those were to be respected.

The Federation of Saint Scholastica took steps to broaden the membership of the Renewal Chapters, to augment chapters with pre-chapters at which agendas would be discussed and set, to issue interim guidelines, and finally to publish an entirely new kind of constitution for the Federation. The story of the procedural developments is counterpointed against the traditional—and still stoutly maintained—autonomy of individual

Benedictine houses. The Renewal Chapters could not order anybody to do anything.

The fifth and final chapter presents analyses of the survey data in several different modes. It attempts to detect the alterations and consistencies in attitudes during a period when behaviors were changing with almost dizzying speed.

The findings overturn any simple characterization of the revolutionaries.

Their attitudes toward their pre-Vatican II life are surprisingly positive. It turns out that qualities they perceived in that style of life have persisted—in some cases have been enhanced—in the outwardly very different style of Benedictine sisters today. The analysis comes to the conclusion that the "it" with which the sisters are "sticking" is, in the ways that count, the "it" with which they began. They have remained faithful—to vows, to tradition, to the church, to self, to each other, to God.

The Federation of Saint Scholastica adopted a new constitution, *Call to Life*. The Rule of Benedict as now understood is a barrier to the reimposition of the pre-Vatican II forms of monastic life.

Benedictine sisters have known for a long time what it is not to be listened to. The patron saint of the Federation, Saint Scholastica, the twin sister of Saint Benedict, tried to get her brother, on one of his visits to her monastery, to take seriously her request that he stay longer for further conversation with her. When he refused, she prayed. The very instant she ended her prayer the rain—good trouble—poured down. Realizing that he could not return home in this terrible storm, Benedict complained bitterly.

"God forgive you, sister!" he said. "What have you done?"

Scholastica simply answered, "When I appealed to you, you would not listen to me. So I turned to my God and God heard my prayer."[15]

part three

Bungee Cord Theology

When considering the "how" of the Benedictine charism in chapter 2, I named "ecumenism" as one of the distinguishing marks.

The term (or its adjectival form, ecumenical) appears seven times in *The Benedict Option*. Five occurrences are in a section called "Reach Across Church Boundaries to Build Relationships" of a chapter titled "The Idea of a Christian Village." Of the remaining two instances, one is in the section "Start Classical Christian Schools" of a chapter called "Education as Christian Formation," about which I will have much to say in Part Four.[1] The seventh occasion is the index.

For Rod Dreher, it's "born in part out of pro-life activism, an 'ecumenism of the trenches,'" involving conservative evangelicals and Catholics. A leader in the Russian Orthodox Church has proposed joining forces in "a 'common front' against atheism and secularism."[2]

Dreher sees evidence of this "ecumenism of the trenches" primarily in the Eighth Day Institute, founded by Erin Doom, employee of a Christian bookstore in Wichita, Kansas. EDI's signature events are the Hall of Men and a subsequently launched parallel women's organization, the Sisters of Sophia. Doom has said, "Ultimately I want to provide tools and resources

for all Christian families to make their homes into little monasteries."[3]

Ecumenism as Dreher portrays it is narrow, reactionary. It
is a joint effort of defiance from "the trenches." For the Benedictines I know, ecumenism makes of their monasteries something very different from Dreher and Doom's paradigm.

The twentieth century saw a 180-degree turn in the Catholic
Church, a reversal that affected Benedictines but that they were
also instrumental in bringing about.

Pope Pius XI, in his 1928 encyclical, *Mortalium Animos,*
codified a fortress mentality when he forbade dialogue and
declared that Christian unity meant unequivocal submission
to the papacy: "So, Venerable Brethren, it is clear why this Apostolic See has never allowed its subjects to take part in the
assemblies of non-Catholics: for the union of Christians can
only be promoted by promoting the return to the one true
Church of Christ of those who are separated from it, for in the
past they have unhappily left it."[4]

Pope Saint John Paul II, in a 1987 address to thirty represen-
tatives of other Christian communities at the University of
South Carolina during his second pastoral visit to the United
States, acknowledged that the fortress has been dismantled and
said there is no going back: "We are definitively committed to
treading the path which the Holy Spirit has opened before us:
the path of repentance for our divisions and of working and
praying for that perfect unity which the Lord himself wishes for
his followers. . . . It is no small achievement of the ecumenical
movement that after centuries of mistrust, we humbly and sin-
cerely recognize in each other's communities the presence and
fruitfulness of Christ's gifts at work."[5]

The revolution marked by John Paul's reversal of Pius's in-
terdict on dialogue is among the most dramatic transformations
in church history. The distance from *Mortalium Animos* to the
Joint Declaration on Justification issued by the Vatican and the
Lutheran World Federation seventy-one years later, in 1999,
defies measurement.

Benedictines have of course been affected by the tectonic shifts in the Catholic Church, especially after Pope Saint John XXIII opened the windows at the Second Vatican Council. However, Benedictines were not just responding to larger forces. They were coming to a fuller grasp of their own Benedictine nature, not unlike Saint John Henry Newman's analysis of the development of doctrine: it "required only the longer time and deeper thought for [its] full elucidation."[6]

Benedictines have taken the lead in ecumenical relationships. They are also in the forefront of interreligious dialogues.

The Benedict Option does not register this fact at all. Dreher makes three brief references to other religions.

- First is a glance at one "doctrinal" claim he sees in what he snidely calls "Moralistic Therapeutic Deism"; "God wants people to be good, nice, and fair to each other, as taught in the Bible and by most world religions."

- Second is a generalized salute: "The sense that the material world discloses the workings of the transcendent order was present in ancient philosophy and in many world religions, even nontheistic ones like Taoism."

- Third is a purely pragmatic directive to Benedict option followers as they prepare to do battle: "Because Christians need all the friends we can get, form partnerships with leaders across denominations and from non-Christian religions."[7]

There are no references to Buddhism or Hinduism, two to radical Islam, and several to Orthodox Jews, whose manner of restricted communal life Dreher acknowledges as a model.

Benedictine options involve other religions in far more profound and formative ways than does the Benedict option; they resonate with the open, hospitable Orthodox Judaism exemplified by the late Lord Jonathan Sacks, chief rabbi of the United Hebrew Congregations of the Commonwealth from 1991 to

2003, who wrote, "Those who are confident in their faith are not threatened but enlarged by the different faith of others."[8]

Benedictine options' engagement with other religions is formalized in Monastic Interreligious Dialogue,

> an international monastic organization that promotes and supports dialogue, especially dialogue at the level of religious experience and practice, between Christian monastic men and women and followers of other religions.
>
> It is a commission of the Benedictine Confederation with formal links to both branches of the Cistercian order. It acts in liaison with the Holy See's Pontifical Council for Interreligious Dialogue and welcomes collaboration with other organizations that foster interreligious dialogue.
>
> While the natural dialogue partners of Christian monastics are monastics of other religious traditions, Monastic Interreligious Dialogue also engages in spiritual dialogue with adherents of religions that do not have an institutionalized form of monasticism, for example—and in particular—with Muslims.[9]

It has been my privilege to be closely associated with Monastic Interreligious Dialogue for three decades. I have seen up close and personal the shifts, both seismic and subtle, that are prompted by encounters across religious lines. Benedictines become different. They report—universally in my experience—that in so doing they become more authentically Benedictine. It's not at all a matter of strategic alliances, nor does it devolve into a least common denominator of "being good, nice, and fair to each other." Because Benedictines know the melody of their own tradition so well, their ear is sensitive to the music in other traditions—their rhythms of practice, their scales of values, their tempo and dynamics of prayer, their dissonances and harmonies with the realities of community.

In the next two chapters I will examine how Benedictines have been especially venturesome in ecumenical and interreligious relations. In both arenas they have expressed what I consider the quintessence of Benedictine options, an image conjured by Father Kilian McDonnell, OSB, in one of his poems: "All our truths need bungee cords."[10] By contrast, the Benedict option prescribes grappling hooks.

chapter five

Other Christians[1]

The ecumenical "how" of the Benedictine charism has sometimes lain dormant.

In the early church, monks were at least as notorious as ecclesiastical shock troops as they were famous as peacemakers. Some of the bitterest disputes between Eastern and Western Christianity have been ignited and fueled by monks. Echoes of Martin Luther's revulsion at his own monastic identity can still be heard in lingering Protestant suspicion of a mode of life about which Luther prayed: "Would to God all monks and nuns would all forsake the cloisters, and thus all the cloisters in the world would cease to exist; this is what I would wish."[2] Monasticism and ecumenism might be thought an unlikely pair.

But denominations matter less than they used to. People are much readier to take seriously the fact that monasticism antedates almost all the major splits in church history. Benedict can be claimed as Our Holy Father by far more than those who have OSB after their names, by even more than the increasing numbers of oblates. The monastery, additionally, has much wisdom to offer the still divided churches on what seeking God together both entails and promises.

Saint John's, the world's largest Benedictine monastery, established in 1967 the Collegeville Institute for Ecumenical and Cultural Research. In so doing, the monks of Saint John's acknowledged that the Rule of Benedict not only permits ecumenism—the Rule positively enjoins it. If the Rule makes the monks ecumenists, the monks in turn impart a special Benedictine spin to ecumenism. The Rule is a charter document of the ecumenical movement.

The Confluence of Traditions

Research during recent decades into the antecedents of the Rule of Benedict has raised a host of doubts about the originality of Benedict. The almost universal conviction now, that his Rule depends on the Rule of the Master, rather than the other way round, has led some scholars to suspect that Benedict, like Jesus in the acid of nineteenth-century historical skepticism, never even existed.

The quest of the historical Benedict is neither easy nor impossible, but as the scope of his originality has diminished, his significance for ecumenism has increased. We now recognize in Benedict a kind of originality rarer and more precious than the out-of-the-blue, bursting-unannounced-upon-the-scene individual inspiration that we prize so highly.

Benedict had two centuries of monastic tradition to draw on. Between Anthony's withdrawal to the desert at the beginning of the fourth century and Benedict's establishment of his community at Monte Cassino at the beginning of the sixth century, tens of thousands of men and women had adopted a dizzying variety of monastic manners of life, each variety a mixture of gospel and cultural influences, all of them appealing in one way or another to the life of the apostles as their model and warrant.

What the Rule of Benedict achieved was nothing less than the discovery of a central tradition in all the accumulated confusion. The crucial ecumenical point is this: the discovery was an act of historical imagination more than of historical research. Benedict knew the sources, to be sure; annotations to *RB1980* are irrefutable evidence of his familiarity with the past. But

Benedict knew that the central tradition was not a statistical mean or the majority opinion. The central tradition could be retrieved—indeed, known—only by persons covenanting together to create a school for the Lord's service (Prol. 45). What the Rule did was to recover a central tradition that has survived and flourished through fifteen centuries. This central tradition is a many-splendored thing, constantly evolving.

We who long for a recovery of a central church tradition amid all the confusion dating back to the sixteenth and eleventh and even earlier centuries would do well to ponder the originality of Benedict's Rule. Tradition will be truly accessible to us only as we commit ourselves to living it together. That "it" has more dimensions than Dreher's Benedict option allows for.

Basis in the Bible

For Protestants, who tend to think of themselves as having a corner on due reverence for biblical authority, the lattice work of biblical citations in the Rule of Benedict is both reassuring and anomalous. Benedict was as fluent in biblical quotation as any proof-texting evangelical in our own day. While some of his scriptural references in support of this or that regulation are strained, he at least believed that Scripture is where you should look to find out what you ought to do.

But the Protestant who is comfortable when viewing a text italicized as often as Benedict's Rule is nevertheless wonders how a form of life apparently so steeped in works-righteousness as Benedictine monasticism can honestly claim a biblical foundation.

It is this anomalous character of the Rule's biblicism that makes Benedict's "back to the Bible" call so significant ecumenically. Like the theological consensus statement of the World Council of Churches Commission on Faith and Order, *Baptism, Eucharist, and Ministry*,[3] the Rule of Benedict goes beyond a catalogue of biblical passages to catch a biblical accent, a way of speaking in which the life of faith can be characterized allusively, in images, rather than in rigid categories.

Moreover, Benedict's Rule is a timely reminder to Protestants that the Bible contains a great deal more than Paul's distinction between law and gospel. The Wisdom tradition, nearly always short shrifted in Protestant spirituality, is retrieved by the Rule and woven into the texture of the Christian life. Benedict reminds us that faith/works is not the only way to slice the gospel pie.

A Lay Community

It was probably no more than a century after the Rule of Benedict was written that most monks were becoming priests. As I noted earlier in chapter 1, this was the most significant transformation in the history of monasticism. Its fundamental importance is reaffirmed again and again as monks resolve and then unresolve not to seek ordination. The gravitational pull of the priesthood is almost irresistible, but there can be no doubt that Benedict conceived his monastery as a lay community.

Provision is made for priests to enter—"If any ordained priest asks to be received into the monastery, do not agree too quickly" (60.1)—and for laymen once entered to become priests (62), but it is clear that Benedict was legislating for the exception. The main point about the priests is that they are to get no special treatment; they are granted no honor in addition to the respect they, like all monks, are due in accordance to the date of entry into the monastery (60.5-7; 62.5, where "the goodness of his life" is the only criterion for advancement). "No one will be excused from kitchen service" (35.1).

If the recovery of serious Bible study provides much of the substance of ecumenical renewal in our time, the reassertion of the lay character of the church constitutes the form of that renewal. Clericalism bedevils all the churches, even those that originated historically in the cry that all believers are priests. The titanic battles over the location of the center of gravity in

Lumen Gentium, Vatican II's Dogmatic Constitution on the Church, can be seen as a macrocosmic expression of the struggle lived in microcosm every day in Benedictine monasteries: Is the church defined by the hierarchy of ordination or by God's election of a people? And the struggle is not limited to monasteries of men. Benedictine sisters are regularly reminded that it is only ordained men who can preside at their Eucharists.

No single action in the twentieth century is so laden with ecumenical potential as the Vatican Council fathers' decision to rest the church on the calling of the people of God. The theme of hierarchy is certainly sounded loud and clear in *Lumen Gentium,* and the persistent overt sexism in the Catholic Church is a sharp reminder of the gap between theory and practice, but in a wide historical perspective the change in theory is nothing short of revolutionary.

Conciliar sanction has been given to the suspicion that the church is in essence a lay community which, if proper precautions are taken, can tolerate priests.

A Family Affair

Benedict is at pains to make sure traveling monks and those who work at a distance will be praying at exactly the same time as the bulk of the community back home (50). He speaks of "the obligations of those who live there" (in the tent of the Lord) (Prol. 39). In many specific instances—for example, meal hours—he lays down regulations and then makes flexibility the overriding rule (37). When the monks are praying the Divine Office, a certain response is "to be said quite deliberately and slowly" to give stragglers time to enter the oratory before the moment at which tardiness obliges punishment (43.4).

In short, the Rule creates primarily a family, only secondarily an institution. The monastery is presented as a place where people dwell together in unity, not always in peace, but always in the conviction that they are in community together for the long haul, for better or for worse, and that they need each other even when they cannot stand each other.

There can be no mistaking the Benedictine family for a modern pop-psychological discussion group in which the parents are nothing more than nondirective enablers. The abbot is in charge. Seldom if ever in the history of legislation has anyone been granted such awesome authority as the Rule of Benedict accords the abbot—but seldom also has any authority been so thoroughly hedged about as is the abbot's by the Rule.

The abbot represents Christ in the monastery (2.2). Benedict's outline of the abbot's role shows an uncanny grasp of the totality of the biblical portrait of Christ: ruler and servant, the one whose authority as ruler derives from identity and action as servant, the one who was made perfect through obedience, who emptied himself.

The tale of efforts to achieve ecumenical reunion by negotiating institutional concordats is a long one, on balance a dreary one. The problem with such enterprises is that they provide no context in which to recover a central tradition. Like arms control negotiations, they tend to deal in "bargaining chips" and are shot through with mutual suspicion. Each party focuses on what it will have to give up, lose, compromise. There is insufficient willingness to pay close attention when an idea emerges that nobody came into the conversation with—a requirement of genuine discernment, as noted in chapter 2.

Reconceiving the ecumenical challenge as the reestablishment of family relationships does not eliminate suspicion. It does, however, shift attention onto what everyone can gain. Families are certainly more than least common denominators—more even than the sum of their parts. The family is a mystery, as Benedict knew.

The recent practice of interim eucharistic fellowship (for example, in the Consultation on Church Union) may have done more than all the theological ink spilled over the last half century to bring real Christian unity closer—or rather, the practice of life together is what finally makes the churches responsive to the theological convergence that says it is all right for Christians to dwell together and wrong for them not to.

Nothing Preferred to Prayer

"Nihil operi Dei praeponatur"—"Nothing is to be preferred to the Work of God" (43.3). Prayer is the Work of God, according to Benedict. Prayer is a focal point of the faith of Christians today.

Faith and Ferment,[4] the thorough study of the state of the churches in Minnesota undertaken by the Collegeville Institute for Ecumenical and Cultural Research and published in 1983, revealed that eighty-two percent of Minnesota Christians pray every day. Some observers of the cultural scene surmise that in this day of science, of cause and effect, of sociological, psychological, anthropological, historical explanation, prayer must surely be on the wane. The evidence is otherwise. It points to the fundamental ecumenical importance of prayer as a common commitment that knows no denominational fences.

Current historiography seeks to take us behind the front-page headlines of the past to the "people" and "lifestyle" sections, to the reconstruction of the textures, atmosphere, and folkways of individual and community life in generations that have preceded ours. Just as future historians of our time who fail to note the widespread practice of prayer among us will not be telling it like it was, so we distort what is past to us if we neglect the tenacious, persistent refusal of Benedictines century after century to prefer anything to the Work of God.

Luther saw the vow as the distinguishing mark of the monk. Because he judged vows to be antithetical to the gospel, he scorned monasticism. According to the Rule of Benedict, however—and in light of actual monastic practice—monastics are identified by what they prefer nothing to—prayer. The monk or sister thus becomes not an ecumenical stumbling block but an ecumenical pioneer.

If the centrality of prayer in the Rule is an ecumenical rallying point, the content of the Work of God further confirms the Rule as an ecumenical charter.

The psalms are at the heart of the whole enterprise. The parts of the Rule of Benedict that put the greatest strain on the patience of those who include the Rule in their programs of *lectio divina* (spiritual reading) are the chapters that go into minute detail about which psalms are to be said in which order on which occasions. Some of these chapters almost drive one into allegorical exegesis. But the spiritual benefit is right there on the surface, in all the boring detail: care must be taken to maintain the Psalter's integrity.

The Psalter of course carries the monk several times a day, every day, year in year out, back to the Bible. Even more, the Psalter in its range and depth charts the spiritual universe more completely than any collection of spontaneous prayers. The psalms remind those who pray them regularly of spiritual concerns far beyond the limits of their own experience and their own immediate worries.

Praying the psalms is precisely the Work of God, not a work we fashion with our own hands and our own intentions. In this Work of God all Christians can learn that just as there are varieties of religious experience, so are there varieties of religious obedience: the confident, the despairing, the joyful, the sorrowing, the content, the angry, the king, the commoner—all these and many more live side by side in the Psalter and acknowledge each other's place in the people of God. Surely one reason monks are ecumenists by instinct at least, maybe even by nature, is that the psalms have ground down the sharp edges of their ecclesiastical exclusivism.

Hospitality

I grew up in a part of the world—Texas—that has a well-deserved reputation for hospitality. When a Texan drawls "Y'all come see us now" to a brand-new acquaintance, the expression is not, as I fear its more insistent but less sincere counterpart in other regions of the country ("You simply *must* come see us sometime") often is, a polite way of ending an awkward conversation. The Texan means it. But Benedictine hospitality is less calculating, more open by far than even the Texan's genuine "Y'all come." The monastery's guests may come uninvited, unannounced, inconvenient.

If, as we saw before, Bible study provides the substance of ecumenical renewal and the lay character of the church provides the form, so also the activity of prayer is ecumenical substance and hospitality is ecumenical form. In our age of media hype it is easy, and often justified, to discount ecclesiastical intervisitation as public relations grandstanding, but welcoming each other in the name of Christ is simply fundamental to the church's way of being the people of God.

Our inability to trust human motives, and our consequent cynicism about hospitality of the ungrudging, no-hidden-agenda Benedictine sort, was made clear when, on hearing some years ago of Israeli Prime Minister Menachem Begin's invitation to President Anwar Sadat of Egypt to visit Jerusalem, most Western observers just could not believe he really meant it. It had to be a trick or a trap. Benedictines were likely the only pundits among us who instinctively knew how to interpret that revolutionary news: Begin and Sadat were writing a chapter in the ancient story of Mediterranean hospitality, not a footnote to a modern manual of diplomatic procedure.

One reason the Benedictines are such good hosts is that they know who they are. The guest is not a threat to their identity. Monastics certainly do not have everything figured out; after all, they have committed themselves to living in a school for the Lord's service where the degree is not granted until the end, and the Rule itself is simply "for beginners" (73.8). They are still on the road, but they know what road they are on.

Deep confusion about Christian identity is documented on page after page of *Faith and Ferment*, the study of Christianity in Minnesota. This confusion may help explain the uneasiness many Christians feel even in the company of other Christians of different traditions, habits, convictions, and priorities. Benedict understood that hospitality and Christian identity are inseparable: hosts must know who they are before they can be good hosts, and they come to know who they are only when they extend hospitality. A paradox—and an ecumenical necessity.

Patience and Urgency

"Already but not yet" is what the Bible tells us about the expression of the will of God in history.

Persons seriously committed to testing their own story against the biblical story find themselves by turn complacent when they should be urgent and hyperactive when they should be patient. What is an authentic Christian experience and stewardship of time? Augustine knew intellectually, and most of us know viscerally, that time is one of the supremely elusive puzzles of our experience. Figuring out what God's "already but not yet" means is surely a task that Christians must work at together, whether we use the fancy language of "eschatology" or inquire plaintively, "Where is this new person I am supposed to be?"[5]

It would be hard to find a more sophisticated meditation on the mystery of God's time than the Rule of Benedict. Many chapters catch the urgency of "the kingdom of God is at hand," while others recommend the patience of those who wait quietly for seeds to germinate and sprout. Benedict knew that time is not only moments of decision but also a continuum through which growth occurs. Love is finally what makes sense of time: "As we progress in this way of life and in faith, we shall run on the path of God's commandments, our hearts overflowing with the inexpressible delight of love" (Prol. 49).

What does it mean to live a Christian life? This question, which we might think must surely have a clear answer after all these centuries, is (and probably always has been, our nostalgia for a "simpler past" notwithstanding) an insistent and troubling enigma—and an ecumenical equalizer, because no one group of Christians has come up with the definitive answer.

The Rule provides ecumenical insight and reassurance because Benedict understands that you do not wait to live the Christian life until you have decided what it is. His sanity and wisdom stand in sharp contrast to both the burnout that often follows an unmodified burst of urgency and the patience that surfaces when boredom extends beyond its appointed time.

Living at the place where "already" meets "not yet" is not particularly comfortable, but that is the place where the gospel puts us. The Rule helps map the territory. The territory is not just "any place," but home. It requires a commitment of stability (4.78; 58.17). The image of ecumenical Christianity is sitting down together at the one banquet table of the Lord.

What and Where Is the Church?

The ecumenical movement is a quest, not a crusade. Our divisions are a scandal, but we overcome them by discovering together a more excellent way. When we ask, "What and where is the church?" we ask the fundamental ecumenical question. We have a chance of finding the answer if we acknowledge that the church is a calling God has set before us.

The quest is not totally in the dark—a great cloud of witnesses surrounds us, and we "run with perseverance the race that is set before us, looking to Jesus the pioneer and perfecter of our faith" (Heb 12:1-2). But even though we have some clues to where we are going, none of us has finished the quest for the church.

The Rule of Benedict is a *vademecum* for those who are on the ecumenical quest.

It demonstrates how, with imagination, a central tradition can be discerned in historical and contemporary confusion.

With unselfconscious ease and naturalness, the Rule of Benedict weaves the biblical revelation into the texture of everyday community and individual life.

Benedict simply assumes that the lay Christian is the normal Christian.

The church is family first and institution only insofar as it must be.

Prayer is at the heart of everything.

Hospitality is of the essence of the gospel life, not a social nicety to be indulged when schedules and resources permit.

The Christian lives urgently and patiently, grounded in stability.

"Unseeable Future"

The graph of the effectiveness of the Rule of Benedict as a charter for ecumenism can be traced in the story of *Worship*, the journal founded in 1926 at Saint John's Abbey by one of the leaders of the liturgical movement, Dom Virgil Michel, OSB. *Worship* is now, at the time of this writing in 2021, at volume 95.

Just two years after the first issue of the journal, Pope Pius XI's *Mortalium Animos*, as I noted in the introduction to Part Three, declared meetings with non-Catholics out of bounds. As late as 1937 *Worship* was blurring the boundary a little, but was still in protective mode. Speaking of the liturgical movement, Dom Virgil wrote, "Already there have been many converts to the true Church as the result of this modern stirring of the Spirit of God; and we Catholics should be the first to rejoice at any intensification of spiritual consciousness in our separated brethren, especially in so far as this invariably leads to some degree of greater approximation to the traditional current of orthodox Catholic Christianity."[6]

This was an advance beyond "A Sermon on Holy Mass" by Fr. Joseph Kreuter, OSB, of Saint John's Abbey, published four years earlier: "Our Protestant brethren cannot grasp the thought that Christ continues to live in His person and in His works in the visible Church. For them Christ is merely the Redeemer who lived nineteen hundred years ago and died for all mankind. All

He did for us is in their eyes only a remembrance or historical fact. They do not believe in a real communion of man with Christ, in an actual presence of Christ in the holy Eucharist."[7]

An article in 1952 registers a change—not so much one that has occurred as one that will. "It has been decided by the Holy See that neither the Catholic Church nor individual Catholics can have any direct part in this organized Ecumenical Movement or be officially represented at and participate in its conferences [the World Council of Churches had been formed four years previously]. . . . The present task is one of preparation: the beginning only of the production of an atmosphere or background wherein minds, hearts and spirits will be ready really— and not merely 'notionally'—to demand and endeavor to implement the uniting of the scattered Christian flocks in an as yet unseeable future."[8]

One adjective, and the horizon expands exponentially: the future is "unseeable." Pope Pius XI certainly saw it—"the uniting of the scattered Christian flocks" would be the penitent and total return to the Roman fold of all who had fallen away. "Unseeable" unlocks the gate for God's "I am about to do a new thing" (Isa 43:19) to sneak in.

In the decades following Vatican II, the list of *Worship* authors becomes itself an ecumenical text—the journal zealously enlisted "the help of Anglican, Orthodox or Protestant scholars." It isn't just authors that broaden the horizon, though. Increasingly, the books chosen for review are by non-Catholics, including some by Jews. It is not uncommon for books by Catholics to be reviewed by non-Catholics.

Celebrating the journal's golden jubilee in 1976, editor Aelred Tegels, OSB, wrote, "Since we appointed the first non-Roman Catholic associate editors in 1967, *Worship* has progressively become more ecumenical in character. At present, with half of the associate editors non-Roman Catholic, with non-Roman Catholic contributors accounting for at least a third of the average issue, and with a substantial percentage of non-Roman

Catholic subscribers, *Worship* can fairly be described as an ecumenical liturgical review."[9]

In the period from Vatican II to today, *Worship* lays out an ecumenical feast. More than 1,800 articles and book reviews include the term "ecumenism" (or "ecumenical").

The flowering of ecumenism in *Worship* is actually foreshadowed in a "Casual Comment" by Dom Virgil in 1929. It turns out that making converts to the liturgy is very like making converts to ecumenism. Yes, people need to change, but the change is not becoming something different. It's becoming more who they already are. "Preach, not by word but by example, by a natural example that reflects the inspiration of your heart, not the artificial example called forth in order to be seen. . . . For the liturgical spirit is just that—a spirit, a fundamental attitude towards the whole of Christian life, which will enter into and lend new and richer spiritual color to every angle of that life."[10]

There is a direct line from Dom Virgil's "new and richer spiritual color" to the most comprehensive and succinct portrayal I have ever seen of the ecumenical spirit. It is a phrase from the 1995 draft of the Joint Declaration on Justification that was signed in 1999 by the Vatican and the Lutheran World Federation: "The diversity between the Lutheran and Catholic understanding of justification is mutually open rather than mutually exclusive."[11]

The Benedict option sees the diversity between Benedictines and the world, in Dreher's reckoning, as mutually exclusive. Benedictine options see the diversity, as I have witnessed it, as mutually open.

chapter six

Other Religions[1]

Historian Arnold J. Toynbee speculated that historians in the future, writing about the twentieth century, will judge the dialogues between Buddhists and Christians more significant than the conflict between democracy and communism.[2] Those dialogues have spilled over into the twenty-first century and are multiplying. It has been my privilege to spend time at that interface. While there, I have perceived a fresh range of Benedictine options.

As a purely astonishing fact, it's hard to top the cultural tenacity of monasticism—Buddhist 2500 years, Christian 1700 years. When Buddhist and Christian monks and sisters get together, time both stands still and explodes. Millennia meet. Monastic Interreligious Dialogue is like a particle accelerator, in which forces interact to reveal primordial conditions, some fundamental features of human nature and human community.

My involvement with Monastic Interreligious Dialogue has been a highlight of my intellectual and spiritual life. I could talk theoretically, as PhDs are carefully trained to do, but I will reflect personally, because you can't spend a lot of time with monastic folks and get away with theory.

Practice is the beginning, practice is the middle, practice is the end of living and knowing both Benedictine and Buddhist. Practice as the key was as revolutionary in fifth-century BCE India and sixth-century CE Italy as in twenty-first-century CE

America. From one perspective, monasticism is supremely countercultural. But taking a long view, we can say that everything else is countercultural, monasticism being the one more-or-less constant through the whole story.

But this more-or-less constant has been in no way static.

"To Live Is to Change"

I begin my reflections in an odd place, with Saint John Henry Newman's recollection, in *Apologia pro vita sua*, of the intellectual turmoil he experienced in 1841 when his famous Tract 90 ignited a firestorm of controversy. The Tract registers movement in his own thought on the relation between Anglican and Catholic doctrine, though it would be four more years before his conversion.

What fascinates me about Newman's recollection is how familiar it sounds, and how germane it is to the encounter between religions: "How was I any more to have absolute confidence in myself? how was I to have confidence in my present confidence? how was I to be sure that I should always think as I thought now?"[3]

In 1841 Newman was afraid that he might not always think as he thought then, yet four years later he would pen one of the most liberating lines ever written, one I quoted at the beginning of this book: "In a higher world, it is otherwise, but here below, to live is to change and to be perfect is to have changed often."[4] This seismic shift in Newman's sensibility, from horror of change to reveling in it, provides a clue to the significance of Monastic Interreligious Dialogue for Benedictine sensibility and, by extension, for the cultural life of the larger world.

I'm mixing metaphors rather haphazardly here, but I don't apologize for doing so, because the realities I'm talking about have so many dimensions, so many valences. I just used seismic shifts. Now I switch to something quieter, more intimate.

Monastic Interreligious Dialogue is like a sitar string which, when plucked in the vicinity of the strings of the Rule of Benedict, elicits vibrations that create wonderful harmonies, as is demonstrated on page after page of a book I edited, *Benedict's Dharma: Buddhists Reflect on the Rule of Saint Benedict*.[5]

I underscore a resonance with what I've always thought the most precious sentence in the Rule, chapter 73's acknowledgment that it is a "little Rule for beginners." The encounter with Buddhist monks and *bhikkhunīs* (female monastics) has been an occasion for Benedictines to move from one stage of beginning to another, from fear of the new to embracing it, to move toward perfection by changing and changing often.

Pope Paul VI did better than he knew when he assigned the initial task of dialogue between Catholics and persons of other religious traditions to Benedictines and Buddhist monastics. He was clearly aware of the many parallels between the monastic ways of life. But I suspect he wasn't thinking about the way Benedictines, more than any other Christians, are capable of rootedness and far-ranging adventure at the same time. I think that Father Kilian McDonnell's image—"All our truths need bungee cords"[6]—is the fruit of his more than half a century of seeking God after the monastic manner of life.

In the conversations that lie behind much of *Benedict's Dharma*, Joseph Goldstein, cofounder of the Insight Meditation Society, said something that resonates with bungee cords: about an idea that had come up, "I want to play with this from another angle. I want to see where it goes." Then he conjured a marvelous image of a Buddhist way of understanding the relation between illusion and reality, saying that our life is like "a movie projected on a screen. All the life is going on up there, but it's only light. It's only light coming through the film."[7]

The specific instance is not as important as the willingness to *play* with an idea. Goldstein's trope resonates with *play* as a theological contribution to interreligious dialogue as it is unforgettably and poignantly registered in the Testament of Dom

Christian de Chergé, one of the Trappist monks killed by extremists at the Monastery of Notre Dame of Atlas in Tibhirine, Algeria, in 1996: "the Spirit whose secret joy will always be to establish communion and restore the likeness, playing with the differences (*en jouant avec les différences*)."[8]

Another way of thinking about Christian truth, very different from bungee cord theology, was expressed by a dear friend and mentor of mine this way: "When I as a Christian sit down in dialogue with someone from another tradition, I know I won't learn anything new." This was not as benighted a statement as it sounds, at least coming from the one who said it, because it presupposes a broad and deep understanding of what constitutes Christian knowledge. But it is not a statement a Benedictine would make.

Adherents of the Rule, who are always at the beginning, expect to learn new things from just about everybody, even from others who are more novice than they; after all, Benedict instructs the abbot to pay particular attention to the youngest in the community (3.3). It works the other way too. In the *Benedict's Dharma* conversations, Judith Simmer-Brown, a Tantric Buddhist layperson and professor at Naropa University, recounted her surprise that Benedict helped her get around some prejudices she had about monasticism in her own tradition.

The Benedictine doesn't just expect to learn new things as in "new information" or "new facts"; the Benedictine expects to learn new things about God, and new ways to think about things both old and new about God. To seek God after the monastic manner of life is truly to seek; it's not just digging around in what you already know.

And you are not afraid to seek God in the company of folks who don't talk about God at all, because you know that God isn't just in talk and sometimes talk is the very last place you should look for God. Practice, practice, practice. If "worship and work" ever goes stale as the Benedictine motto, they might adopt or adapt a remark of legendary golfer Gary Player: "The more I practice, the luckier I get."

The Gethsemani Encounter

In 1996 I had a genuinely unique privilege, an assignment that no one in the prior history of the world ever had. I was asked by Monastic Interreligious Dialogue to be the interface between the fifty monastics, half of them Christian and half of them Buddhist (including His Holiness the Dalai Lama), and the hundred observers at the Gethsemani Encounter, a week-long joint exploration of spiritual traditions and life, where papers were read but, more important, prayers were prayed and meditations meditated and silence kept and pilgrimages walked through the cemetery and trees planted.

One of my responsibilities was to meet with the observers and gather their questions to relay to the monastic participants. One consequence of all this was my subsequently suggesting to Monastic Interreligious Dialogue that they sponsor a book of reflections by Buddhists on the Rule of Benedict. I ended up editing *Benedict's Dharma*.

The puzzlements of observers at the Gethsemani Encounter, who were fascinated by what might be happening when Buddhists and Christians really get to know one another, serve as hints for what Monastic Interreligious Dialogue means for Benedictine culture—for the continued development and expansion of Benedictine options.

The most striking feature of what the observers wondered about is their recognition that experience would provide the only satisfactory answers. They didn't want theoretical speculation. Rather, they asked: "What is the *practical* difference between the Buddhist focus on self-perfection and the Christian aim to grow in likeness to Christ?" Or, to take the shadow side: "In the name of religion much suffering has been inflicted on humanity. How do you deal with the legacy of harm your tradition has done?" Note that the monastics were not asked, "How does *your tradition* deal with the legacy of harm?" but "How do *you* deal with it?" And the most personal question of all, cutting through all abstractions, getting to the heart of the matter: "We would like to hear from the dialoguers' *personal* experience. What do you do when you pray, and how does it feel? Did you have a moment at which the experience 'clicked,' when you realized 'this is it'? Have you had an experience in which you realized you were hitting common ground with the experience of people in other religions, when you could say to one another, 'I feel my prayer is meeting your prayer'?"

The Gethsemani Encounter highlighted, italicized, and bold-faced a truth that outsiders instinctively understood: monastic culture really is a culture; it is about formation of whole persons; it is about recognition and realization more than it is about argument and logic; it is testimony that Keats was at least close to right when, in "Ode on a Grecian Urn," he made beauty and truth interchangeable—though both the Buddha and Benedict acknowledge that there is much, in the monastery as well as outside, that is neither true nor beautiful.

The questions occasionally were more abstract—I categorized them as "theoretical (comparative)"—but even they had a practical edge. "How does each tradition try to make the case for asceticism in today's hedonistic, instant-gratification culture?" We asked the monastics whether they would "compare their frustrations—Buddhist frustrations and Christian frustrations—in the effort to make their messages effective in the larger society"?

Given Western discomfort with the inherited notion of sin and fascination with Eastern alternatives, in one of the questions, which on the surface sounds like it was lifted from an undergraduate introductory religious studies course exam, you can hear the rumblings of cross-cultural tectonic plate encounter: "How are good karma and bad karma and the mitigation of bad karma similar to and different from virtue and sin and forgiveness?" I suppose the fundamentalist answers would be, from the Christian side, that to talk of karma is sin, and from the Buddhist side, that to be burdened by the notion of sin is the result of bad karma.

But monastics don't waste time in such carping; rather, they wonder what they can learn from each other. The observers wondered how much of this was happening in both directions: "Is Buddhism being changed by its contact with Christianity as Christianity is being affected by contact with Buddhism—for example, through the adoption/adaptation of meditation techniques?" "What does it mean to be a Catholic practicing Buddhist practices?" *We each have a piece of the*

These questions would have made the Newman of "How can I be confident?" shudder, but the Newman of "to live is to change and to be perfect is to have changed often" would have found them congenial. *truth?*

He might even have welcomed a conversation with Diana Eck, who on the last day of the Gethsemani Encounter etched a fundamental question as sharply as it can be put. "I am so well aware as a Christian—as we bow deeply in the choir and talk about that which is, which was, which ever shall be—that it is precisely this language that our Buddhist brothers and sisters pull out from under our feet, in some way, as they invite us into reflection on change, on the impermanence of the world in which we live, so that we might change it and ourselves for the better."[9]

I would add that it's when the ground is suddenly not there that the Benedictine is especially glad to have truths attached to bungee cords.

The hundred observers were a mixed lot, though as was to be expected in the American context, there was a predominance of Christians, and they had some probing questions for the Buddhists. "Are the issues raised by feminism being addressed in Buddhism? Is women's experience changing Buddhism, in theory and/or in practice?" A radical question, to be sure, but not as radical as this: "We would like to hear an ecumenical discussion among the Buddhist participants. Do different Buddhist traditions—for example, those that depend on classical texts and those that do not—result in different experiences of Buddhism? Do all Buddhist traditions acknowledge the full authenticity of all the others?" I frankly don't recall whether either of these questions was addressed directly by the participants, but my point is to illustrate the quality of cultural awareness and probing that comes naturally when monastics are sharing their experiences of the spiritual life, or rather, of life itself.

When Benedictine and Buddhist monastics meet, they practice *their life*. The memories that are evoked in both communities—memories that extend back for centuries and centuries—are reminders that a distinction between "spiritual life" and "life" is artificial.

No greater spiritual worth resides inherently in scholarship than in woodworking or kitchen service. It is precisely the ordinariness of scholarship—its being a *labora* that is no closer to *ora* than is any other task—that guarantees its survival. As Abbot Jerome Theisen, OSB, of blessed memory, once said to another abbot, "I'll trade you three theologians for one plumber."

In the brief introductory paragraph to the list of questions the observers at Gethsemani presented to the participants, we said, "We recognize we are enormously privileged to be attending an event that is a very big deal (but of course no big deal at all!)." That "no big deal at all" has a characteristic Buddhist ring, but its resonance with "little Rule for beginners," and of course with the steps of humility (7.10-70), means it is also a Benedictine insight.

I have for a long time thought that God has a sense of humor, the sort that is hidden in Benedict's restrictions on laughter, because there are few things funnier than the disorientation of someone who visits a monastery expecting to find a bunch of holy people doing spiritual things. This is a feature of Buddhist monastic life too. Norman Fischer, a Zen priest, said in the *Benedict's Dharma* conversations, "I think you know you're in a room full of spiritual practitioners when someone begins a story, 'It was the worst . . .' and then goes on from there."

Fischer also said, "I actually found the Rule of Benedict to be much more useful than Dogen's rule [by which he lives] because

Benedict by comparison is very practical and kind-hearted and personal." Joseph Goldstein immediately added, "and allows a half bottle of wine a day." The reference is to Saint Benedict's famous remark, "With due regard for the infirmities of the sick, we believe that a half bottle of wine a day is sufficient for each" (40.3).

Brother David Steindl-Rast, OSB, who would eventually write the Epilogue to *Benedict's Dharma*, immediately noted, "Nobody knows what a *hemina* [the Latin term translated 'a half bottle'] was, and they probably didn't even know in Benedict's day how much wine that was." Then Fischer said, "In Buddhism there's no wine." Judith Simmer-Brown retorted, "That's true of some parts of Buddhism but not mine." This interchange between Fischer and Goldstein and Simmer-Brown reinforced my conviction that there is no such thing as Buddhism or Christianity—they are only abstractions. There are Buddhists and there are Christians. There may be as many Buddhisms and Christianities as there are adherents of each.

Most Benedictines, I suspect, would claim—or at least would like to claim—as their own this wisdom of Vietnamese Buddhist Thich Nhat Hanh: "The dishes themselves and the fact that I am here washing them are miracles!"[10] It is possible to read "No one will be excused from kitchen service" (35.1) as meaning drudgery is an equal opportunity employer, but what Nhat Hanh's Zen insight illuminates is that no one should be excluded from an arena where God can be found.

The significance of Monastic Interreligious Dialogue for Benedictine culture is in fact a huge paradox—which is hardly surprising, since paradox is the natural habitat for the profoundly human. The most searching question asked by the observers at Gethsemani is finally unanswerable, because the very posing of the question begs the further question of how you could ever know whether your answer is correct: "Is it possible to *understand* the other without *experiencing* her/his reality?" I suspect I'm not unique in having wanted to scream "No you don't!" when someone has tried to comfort me with "I know *just* how you feel." We can't ever be sure that we understand the other.

Ground Zero — *Eucharist is transformative*

But we can be confident that the encounter with the other enhances—even if it does not exhaust—our understanding of ourselves. In a wry, all-too-true observation, C. S. Lewis's Screwtape, the senior devil, advises his nephew, the junior devil Wormwood, on how to capture someone: "You must bring [the patient] to a condition in which he can practice self-examination for an hour without discovering any of those facts about himself which are perfectly clear to anyone who has ever lived in the same house with him or worked in the same office."[11]

The work on *Benedict's Dharma* itself unveiled a truth about options. At the beginning of the project there was an assumption on my part—probably on that of many people involved— that it would be about the Rule of Benedict, and along the way we would insert some pointers to how this could be useful for laypersons. As the project went on, it became clear that this was a totally artificial line of demarcation. *All* of it was about how the Rule is of use to *anybody*.

Brother David noticed the Buddhist appreciation for different kinds of temperaments—that is, there is this kind of Buddhism for this kind of person, that kind of Buddhism for that kind of person. On first impression this might seem to contrast with a supposed gravitational pull in Christianity toward some notion that everybody ought to be the same, the same pattern ought to work for everyone. But as I have insisted throughout this book, the Rule, supplemented by stories of fifty generations of Benedictines, appreciates the varieties of people and the varieties of modes of life that are appropriate for them.

Norman Fischer said, "I can either leave the world into the monastery, or leave from the monastery into the world, through

ritual gates." Instead of material walls and gates around monasteries, there are ritual walls and gates that are permeable—very
like Brother Cadfael's medieval home. When I heard Fischer say
this, what immediately came to mind was the most compelling
instance of open-ended monastic options that I know of. It's not
Benedictine, but I have heard Benedictines say similar things.

It's the directive that Father Zosima gives to novice Alyosha
in *The Brothers Karamazov*—he sends him "into the world."
Alyosha wonders why: "Here [in the monastery] was quiet, here
was holiness, and there—confusion, and a darkness in which
one immediately got lost and went astray."[12] Alyosha's choice is
not the Benedict option, but one of many Benedictine options—
to live *in the darkness*, which Father Zosima knew was already
flooded with light.

The occasion for my rereading the transcript of the conversations that lie behind *Benedict's Dharma* was my preparing to
introduce the Buddhist contributors at a conference organized
to celebrate publication of the book. It was held at Our Lady of
Grace Monastery in Beech Grove, Indiana, September 21–23,
2001. What had happened ten days earlier was of course at the
front of everyone's consciousness. Travel restrictions meant
that some participants were unable to come.

In the record of a conversation that had taken place almost
two years earlier, two passages stunned me. Joseph Goldstein:
"If we think of awareness as at the ground, everything serves
that—ground zero is awareness. Out of it grow many different
trellises and plants. It's interesting to see how culturally influ-
enced the different forms are, some being the very elaboration
of the ritual, some being very stripped down, almost no ritual."
Then, just a few minutes later, Brother David Steindl-Rast: "In
the Benedictine tradition, listening would be ground zero."

After citing these two quotations, I concluded my introduction: "We are here at ground zero, at this ground zero, for awareness and listening." Benedictine options and Buddhist options
came into focus.

The literature of ecumenism, the subject of the previous chapter, is peppered with acknowledgments that dialogue has increased participants' understanding of and appreciation for their own traditions. The change that occurs often doubles back on itself, turning out to be a deeper commitment to what you started with.

On the final day at Gethsemani some of us were asked to comment on what had most struck us. I can recall what I said only because it got recorded and is in the Gethsemani Encounter book. "For me, the question, 'What was most surprising here?' had its threshold set by [Zen abbot] Norman Fischer's remark that he had discovered here how much Christians love Jesus. I found that an extraordinary statement! I too felt that the depth, the sincerity and the persuasion with which people talked about their love of Jesus was something that I have not heard in any Christian setting at that degree in quite a long time."[13]

In his classic book, *The Love of Learning and the Desire for God*, Jean Leclercq, OSB, declared that "if the great ideas of the past are to remain young and vital, each generation must, in turn, think them through and rediscover them in their pristine newness."[14] Monastic Interreligious Dialogue has provided for current Benedictines an extraordinarily effective means for that thinking through and rediscovery.

At the head of the list of fresh insights is the way the Buddhists of *Benedict's Dharma* noticed how positive Benedict is about human nature and its prospects. As I wrote at the end of the introductory chapter: "Neither the Buddha nor Benedict was gloomy, and Buddhists reflecting on the Rule help to illuminate the ancient and tenacious—though often submerged—Christian understanding that our fundamental nature is not darkness but light. Benedict, like the Buddha, wants us to wake up."[15]

Benedictines by their very DNA are predisposed to adventure, to expecting that they won't always think as they think now. While they know, as Father Kilian has stated perfectly, if I may say so, in his poem "Perfection, Perfection,"[16] that perfection is not a goal but a trap—hence they don't expect change to take them all the way—they are connoisseurs of change. They cast their lot—or do their bungee jump—with the Newman of 1845: "to live is to change, and to be perfect is to have changed often."

Benedictines are credited with saving civilization in the Middle Ages by the patient copying of manuscripts. The stage has been set in our time by the relentless encounter of customs and religions and languages and worldviews, in face of which many people are afraid and respond by losing heart or becoming defensive, even shrill. I'm counting on Benedictines to help save civilization in the twenty-first century by their example of a culture of trust, not fear. Saving civilization is not at all the same thing as saving the West.

As I think about the overall effect of Monastic Interreligious Dialogue for the perpetuation and flourishing of Benedictine culture, I suggest that Benedictines make one emendation to the Rule: chapter 55, on "Clothing and Footwear," should add to a monastic's necessities, after "two cowls and two tunics," "one bungee cord."

part four

The World of Many Colors

As Rod Dreher sifts through the levels of what he sees as "a world growing cold, dead, and dark," he finds at bottom "anthropological error." "An anthropology," he says, is "an idea of what a human being is."[1]

As with *the* West and *the* Christian tradition, Dreher claims there is "the religious model of the human person," and refers to a fixed thing called "the Bible's anthropology."[2]

I certainly agree that our understanding of anthropology, or, more colloquially, what sort of critters we are, is of fundamental importance in deciding how we should be and what we should do.

In our "Western tradition" we have been variously defined as rational animals, featherless bipeds, the measure of all things, as forked sticks, what we eat, such stuff as dreams are made on, a hybrid of ape and angel. The Bible says that we are made in the image of God, a little lower than the angels, that we are dust and ashes, that we fade as the flower of the field, that we are worms.

There are many religious models of the human person. Biblical anthropology itself is not a closed system.

It is not an exaggeration to say that for Dreher the clinching argument for the Benedict option is sex, specifically the threats of gay marriage and transgenderism. Page after page of his book is devoted to these topics.

The gist is this: "Gay marriage and gender ideology signify the final triumph of the Sexual Revolution and the dethroning of Christianity because they deny Christian anthropology at its core and shatter the authority of the Bible."[3] Apart from the theologically dodgy image of "dethroning," this sentence rules out of Christian identity churches that have concluded, on theological and biblical grounds, that the gay and transgender communities are not denying Christian anthropology but are in fact deepening it.

Dreher explicitly draws the line: "Sexual practices are so central to the Christian life that when believers cease to affirm orthodoxy on the matter, they often cease to be meaningfully Christian."[4] It seems he excludes from the category of "meaningfully Christian" the majority of American Catholics, who support same-sex marriage.[5]

Dreher simply cannot believe that a church believes it is a church if it deviates from his view of what a church believes. He attributes what he caricatures as "watering down or burying biblical truth on sexuality" to a cynical marketing ploy "for the sake of keeping Millennials"—"Mainline Protestant churches have tried this strategy, and they remain in demographic collapse."[6]

Dreher doesn't limit his argument to "the biblical truth of sexuality." He appeals to "the structure of reality itself" and "the givenness of nature." "Is the natural world and its limits a given," he asks rhetorically, "or are we free to do with it whatever we desire?" Nature, for him—indeed, reality itself—is defined by the Bible as he reads it. According to his interpretation of the nature of reality, the desire Dreher feels for his wife is legitimate; the desire that Pete Buttigieg feels for his husband is illegitimate. He classifies the former as among "the facts of our biology." He scorns the latter as "whatever."[7]

He grounds the "givenness of nature" even more deeply when he says that "marriage has to be sexually complementary because only the male-female pair mirrors the generativity of the divine order."[8] To restrict mirroring "the generativity of the divine order" to sexual reproduction is, in my view, an almost blasphemous limiting of God's creativity. Surely when Benedict saw "all that lay beneath God" he saw more generativity than Adam and Eve copulating.

Psychological discovery that gender is in fact fluid—that gay persons are not simply "expressing a preference" and transgender persons are not haphazardly deciding "whatever the choosing individual wants [gender] to be"—is in Dreher's view simply evidence that "Psychological Man won decisively and now owns the culture—including most churches."[9] But science tells me a lot about "the givenness of nature"—hence, about God. When in 1973 the American Psychiatric Association removed homosexuality from the *Diagnostic and Statistical Manual of Mental Disorders*, a move endorsed two years later by the American Psychological Association, I learned something about nature. I do not believe that these two professional associations "sold out" to a hedonistic culture that is locked in a life-or-death struggle with true Christians.

The "natural world" is far more various and far less delimited than those who wrote the Bible knew. The universe is vaster; slavery is not a cornerstone of social order; women's subordination to men has been called out (at least in some realms) as misogyny; the connection of human beings to the rest of the world, encoded in our DNA, is intricate beyond even our best understanding so far.

I do not see justification for separating out sexuality as immune to new comprehension. Dreher believes anyone who thinks like this has succumbed to what he calls a "modern repaganization" and is therefore not a Christian.[10] In the thirteenth century the bishop of Paris, seconded by the archbishop of Canterbury, thought the same about Thomas Aquinas's incorporation of Aristotle.

While Dreher obsesses about the sexual revolution, seeing it as symptomatic of something even deeper, related to the triumph of "Psychological Man," the real culprit in his cultural whodunit, the villain that has dealt the death blow, is the self, "the ever-changing Self that is seeking liberation from all limits and unchosen obligations."[11]

He puts it starkly: "In the end, either Christ is at the center of our lives, or the Self and all its idolatries are." This is followed immediately by what I cited in the opening of Part One: "There is no middle ground." A couple of paragraphs earlier he has specified "what is radical about Saint Benedict's life: total abandonment of the self-will for the will of God."[12]

There is some fuzziness here. The implied parallelism is Christ vs. self and will of God vs. self-will, but these are not readily interchangeable. Christ is not identical to will of God, self is not identical with self-will. It is these sharp, no middle ground polarities that undergird Dreher's single Benedict option.

Benedictines, as I know them, aren't nearly so bifurcated. They inhabit a middle ground, room to move around in, to explore. The Rule doesn't exalt the self—but doesn't denigrate it either. Christ at the center of one's life is more like what Benedict saw in his vision than like what Benedict was seeking when he fled Rome.

"Either Christ or the Self." On the matter of anthropology, Dreher's Benedict option is like a transistor in a digital computer—it's either one or zero. There is "Psychological Man" or there is a Christian.

Benedictine options are like a quantum computer, working in qubits, that can be one and zero simultaneously. Benedictines whom I know realize how many dimensions there are to psychology. "What Would Jesus Do?" is a real question, not the answer to one.

Dreher's view of society and community follows directly from his anthropology.

He quotes with approval an email sent to him by conservative radio talk host Michael Medved: " 'Make sure you live in a community that shares your faith and your values. When your child leaves home to go play with the neighborhood kids, you have to be able to trust that the values in your home are not under-mined by the company he keeps.'"[13]

The practical consequence? The Benedict option becomes a sequestering in the company of the like-minded, a kind of ideological redlining, a sort of gated community of orthodox Christians for whom "orthodoxy" is strictly defined—mainly in its views about sex. It's as if the "more perfect union" envisioned by the US Constitution is like the ideal of the Donatists, discussed in chapter 3: a moated fortress with the drawbridge pulled up—the exact opposite of the twelfth-century monastery of Brother Cadfael, at the center of the community.

Dreher might counter that the entire community in medieval times was centered on God, but Ellis Peters's persuasive portrayal of that period makes clear that there were many competing notions of who God is and what God wants. The monks kept company with people who didn't share their values—they were ecumenists even then—and not all the monks were of one mind either.

The Benedict option as a homogeneous zone is, at best, only one option among many. I believe it isn't a genuine Benedictine option at all.

To his credit, Dreher chalks up some of what he calls the enfeeblement of orthodox Christians to their misplaced confidence in "Republican politicians and the judges they appoint." Why is this a mistake? "The deep cultural forces that have been separating the West from God for centuries will not be halted or reversed by a single election, or any election at all."[14] Dreher's warning was certainly not heeded at the 2020 Republican National Convention, where Donald Trump was hailed as "the bodyguard of Western civilization."

The problem with Dreher's kind of talk is in its premise: that the West has been separated from God.

Yes, God-talk of the sort that comes naturally to Dreher is out of fashion, but that doesn't automatically mean that God has been banished. It simply means that some ways of talking about God have been sidelined or dismissed, often for good theological reasons.

What Dreher holds up as traditional orthodoxy is not all there is to tradition. For instance, Richard Rohr's "Universal Christ"[15] is not the consequence of "deep cultural forces . . . separating the West from God." It's the outcome of Benedict's seeing all that lies beneath God, of Newman's "to live is to change." As Jesus said, "I still have many things to say to you, but you cannot bear them now." It is "the Spirit of truth" who "will guide you into all the truth" (John 16:12-13). Rohr's subtitle is *How a Forgotten Reality Can Change Everything We See, Hope For, and Believe.* The key term here is "forgotten"—it's not something dreamed up just now.

Dreher's prescription of the homogeneous neighborhood is not without nuance. He cites with approval the late Czech dissident, Václav Benda who, while refusing all collaboration with the Communists, "rejected ghettoization."[16]

Following Benda's lead, "dissident Christians should see their Benedict Option projects as building a better future not only for themselves but for everyone around them." They should be, as the monks of Norcia are, "like a Marine Corps of the religious life, constantly training for spiritual warfare," but they should also be, as one of the Norcia monks put it, "as open to the world as they can be without compromise." This same monk went on to say, "It's a lot easier to help people see their own goodness and then bring them in than to point out how bad they are and bring them in."[17]

Yes, but perhaps they are good in a way that the orthodox Christian doesn't recognize. Maybe they have more gifts to give than to receive. It's not a foregone conclusion that they need to be "brought in." The implied parallel between the Czech Communist party and LGBTQ "allies" makes it easy for Dreher to draw sharp lines. He says that a company's asking employees to become "allies" of LGBTQ colleagues "would be the modern equivalent of burning a pinch of incense before a statue of Caesar."[18]

Despite Dreher's acknowledgment that, as one of his anonymous sources put it, "It's easy to fall into the trap of thinking that everybody outside the community is corrupt, but it's not true,"[19] there is one realm of society that Dreher thinks is corrupt through and through.

"Because public education in America is neither rightly ordered, nor religiously informed, nor able to form an imagination devoted to Western civilization, it is time for all Christians to pull their children out of the public school system."[20] Note the uncompromising term: *all.*

"Today our education system fills students' heads with facts, with no higher aspiration than success in worldly endeavor," Dreher says. To claim that America's public schoolteachers are devoid of concern for the moral, ethical, social justice, civilizing dimensions of their work, that they encourage in their students "no higher aspiration than success in worldly endeavor," that there has been a total break from "the pursuit of virtue,"[21] is nothing short of slander. Some of the most serious and sustained attention to values and character in this country happens every day in our public schools.

Dreher's unsparing indictment of public education is the most unjustified of all his prescriptions for the Benedict option. I know of very few, if any, actual Benedictines who would come anywhere close to leveling such a censure. Most would roundly disavow it.

How would Dreher account for the actions of the students at Marjory Stoneman Douglas High School following the Valentine's Day massacre there in 2018? Yes, if those seventeen friends had been pulled out of the public school system they wouldn't be dead, but the ones who were left alive responded in a way that I consider demonstrates the very best of the "Christian tradition of the West," even if some of them, maybe most of them, wouldn't put it in those terms.

Emma González doesn't measure up to Dreher's sexual model, but I thank God for her—for who and how she is, and for the formation she has had in the public schools. In my judgment, she has taken several Benedictine options.[22]

Dreher champions what he calls "classical Christian schools," where "the Western canon" is presented "in a systematic fashion that's deeply integrated into a Christian anthropology and a comprehensive vision of reality."[23]

To be sure, there is wisdom in the canon. Christian tradition has many things to say about anthropology and society. But, as Hamlet cautions, "There are more things in heaven and earth, Horatio, Than are dreamt of in your philosophy" (Act 1, Scene 5). I would place Dreher's orthodox Christianity among the philosophies than which there are more things—including additional Christian things. But "classical Christian schools" leave out so much.

Dreher sees our time as out of joint. I certainly don't counter with a Panglossian "best of all possible worlds," but when an analysis of our condition entails all Christians pulling their children out of the public school system, the condition itself has been seriously misconstrued.

Dreher's Benedict option is suited to "a world growing cold, dead, and dark" that he finds himself in, the world like the one he sees Benedict "turn his back on." Benedictine options are for a world of many colors, the many colors that make up the ray of light Benedict saw the world gathered up into.

The next two chapters tell of Benedictine options in the middle ground, where monastics and the rest of us live.

chapter seven

Sea Ebbs, Bell Clangs[1]

In 1990 I was asked to address the American Benedictine Academy. I observed that a non-monastic's coming before them and pretending to illuminate their life was curious, even presumptuous.

"If I have any warrant," I declared, "it comes from Abbot Jerome Theisen, OSB, of Saint John's Abbey who, writing to thank me for a presentation copy of the book Donald Swearer and I wrote, *For the Sake of the World: The Spirit of Buddhist and Christian Monasticism*,[2] said, 'We appreciate your presence in our midst and your enthusiasm for the monastic life [which] often exceeds our own understanding of it!'"

"Had I stood here a year ago," I said, "and told you that by now the Berlin Wall would be down, Germany united, and an imprisoned Catholic playwright elected president of Czechoslovakia, that Nelson Mandela would have addressed the United States Congress, and that the president of the Soviet Union would have received and accepted an invitation to a NATO meeting, you would have scoffed."

My point was one that was made classically by the great historian of Victorian England, G. M. Young: "The first lesson of history, and it may well be the last, is that you never know what is coming next."[3]

"You Never Know What Is Coming Next"

"If I stand here now," I continued, "and tell you that in ten years, at the beginning of the third millennium of the Christian era, monasticism will be flourishing, vocations will be on the rise, and the stories of monks and sisters will be bestsellers as Thomas Merton's *The Seven Storey Mountain* was half a century earlier, you will disbelieve. I am not going to tell you that. I heed H. L. Mencken's warning that 'the prophesying business is like writing fugues; it is fatal to everyone save the [person] of absolute genius.'"[4] Then I talked about my identity as a historian: "My whole training has been in making sense of the past. I have taken a vow to the discipline of the footnote, and you cannot footnote the future. But I have accepted this assignment to speak about what is to come, and while I cannot fulfill my obligation with authority, I hope to do so responsibly."

At the time, 1990, retreat and retrenchment seemed apt descriptions of the monastic condition. Fewer and fewer sisters and monks were left upon the shore as the monastic ebb tide receded farther and farther into the distance and into the past. But I took great comfort in the tally of the movement's previous obituaries.

There have been people, Christians and non-Christians alike, who, were they to have come back from the dead and seen the group I was standing before, would have been puzzled, even scandalized. The church and the world were supposed to have grown beyond such outmoded, world-hating, life-constricting obsessions. The seeds of anti-monasticism, planted centuries before, came to full growth in the aftermath of the French Revolution, and were classified in Marx's claim that poverty is no virtue, Freud's that chastity is neurotic, and Nietzsche's that obedience is a trait of slaves.

Yet here these late-twentieth-century Benedictines were, in no obvious way more beset by pathologies than their non-monastic contemporaries. "Indeed," I said, "the burden of my talk is your sanity that exceeds most people's understanding of it. A paleographer a few centuries from now, coming across a copy of this address, might conjecture: 'Surely the speaker said, "The burden of my talk is your *sanctity*," and the letters "ct" have simply dropped out of this line of transmission of the text, leaving the improbable reading "sanity." ' But what I say is what I mean. There have been moments in history, to be sure, when sanctity has had to challenge sanity head-on, but ours is a time when sanity and sanctity are virtually indistinguishable, and both in perilously short supply."

Rod Dreher makes much use of the image "liquid modernity." He notes that Zygmunt Bauman's 2000 book of that title draws a distinction between " 'solid modernity'—a period of social change that was still fairly predictable and manageable"—and " 'liquid modernity,' our present condition, in which change is so rapid that no social institutions have time to solidify."[5] I'm not persuaded that earlier times were that much more solid than ours. Literature from previous centuries reflects a lot of unpredictability. G. M. Young's "you never know what is coming next" applies—to varying degrees, to be sure—to all times and all places.

But the liquid image is suggestive. It puts me in mind of the sea.

To see monasticism in perspective, I look at it from two points, two images, fixed by poets. The first image is from Matthew Arnold's "Dover Beach," published in 1867.

At a time when many cultural pundits were celebrating humanity's release from the shackles of religious tradition, Arnold, who was convinced traditional religion was irretrievable, recorded in haunting lines his sense of regret, of melancholy, of lost treasure:

> The sea of faith
> Was once, too, at the full, and round earth's shore
> Lay like the folds of a bright girdle furl'd;

But now I only hear
Its melancholy, long, withdrawing roar,
Retreating to the breath
Of the night-wind down the vast edges drear
And naked shingles of the world.

The poem concludes with a picture of such stark gloom that it might be taken as a prophecy of the twentieth century, the most violent the world has yet known:

And we are here as on a darkling plain
Swept with confused alarms of struggle and flight,
Where ignorant armies clash by night.[6]

There is still a lot of faith around, a century and a half after Arnold registered its retreat, but there is a widespread suspicion that Arnold was basically right: faith is in ebb tide, and culture and politics are counterpointed against that melancholy, long, withdrawing roar. The suspicion is codified in Rod Dreher's portrayal of our world as "growing cold, dead, and dark."

But the sea has depths beneath the tides. Another poet, more recently, fixes the second point from which I see monasticism and its prospects.

In 1922 T. S. Eliot portrayed in "The Waste Land" a world drained of all color, all vitality: there was only dryness, a desolation at least as hopeless as that of Arnold's darkling plain:

A heap of broken images, where the sun beats,
And the dead tree gives no shelter, the cricket no relief,
And the dry stone no sound of water.[7]

"The deep sea swell" appears in "The Waste Land," but in a section called "Death by Water." It is in 1941, after Eliot's conversion to Christianity, that water, in "The Dry Salvages," the third of his "Four Quartets," becomes an image of life and of hope, as the motion of the sea brings not death but stability, a reference point in the mist of space and time:

And under the oppression of the silent fog
The tolling bell
Measures time not our time, rung by the unhurried
Ground swell, . . .

And the ground swell, that is and was from the beginning,
Clangs
The bell.[8]

I believe the sound of monasticism in our day, and for the future in which our hopes and fears meet, is the groundswell's bell pealing over the ebbing sea's roar. That bell peals options, not simply one that says "withdraw."

Hearing the Bell

How does it happen that I hear this bell?

First, as a historian I keep stumbling over monastics. Whether I am roaming in the ancient world, the modern, the medieval, the Renaissance, I find men and women living the vowed life in community. I can delve even farther—a whole millennium farther—into the past in Asia and find monks all over the place, as they are still today.

There is more than a little touch of what C. S. Lewis called "chronological snobbery"[9] in the claim, whether made in anti-monastic jubilation or in pro-monastic despair, that the plight of monasticism today is uniquely grave, even terminal. Through all the changes and chances to which human nature has been subject—*homo classicus, homo medievalis, homo illuminatus, homo modernus*, and whether the sea of faith was at full flood or low ebb—the reality of *homo monasticus* has persisted. Nothing seems to last very long these days; by its persistence monasticism is, ironically, a novelty.

So: first I hear the groundswell's bell because no matter what the cultural barometric pressure, no matter whether the tide is coming in or going out, monasticism is there. Things come, things go, and through it all, there's the monastery. But species do become extinct. The ebbing sea's roar is loud. Why do I hear the bell sharp and clear, not faint and retreating?

People are tired of fragments, of divisions. Two images from 1989—East and West Germans dancing atop the Berlin Wall and the lone Chinese protester confronting the line of tanks in Tiananmen Square—serve as icons, not only for Germany and China, of a world longed for and a world dreaded. The world that is longed for is one that monks and sisters know something about. To say that monasticism's sound resonates with hopes pent up for generations and recently let loose in the world is to make a large claim.

It is a claim I make. Here is why.

The Humpty Dumpty of our common life is shattered. On this point I pretty much agree with Rod Dreher. Who did it, when it happened, whether it was by accident or malicious intent or inattention—we could tell tales for days on end and we would not agree. The point is not how or why, but the way most efforts to clean up the mess have only made it worse.

We have specialized in analysis of the fragments and have mistaken single-mindedness for commitment, so that we fight to have our fragment most prominently displayed, in the best light. "My analysis of my fragment provides the key for reconstructing the whole Humpty Dumpty." Meanwhile quietly, without fanfare or fuss, monks and sisters have been doing what all the king's horses and all the king's men, in their frenzy and in their shouting, have not managed: putting the world together again—by employing many options.

Here I present what I see as monasticism's wisdom, the groundswell's bell, in terms taken from academic discourse. I do this not because I think it is the best language; later I will explicitly say I think it is not. Academic talk is at least as much part of the problem of fragmentation as it is part of the solution. But it is terminology familiar to me, and I do rather enjoy using academic categories to undermine academic categories. I believe monastic experience solves, or at least hints at solutions to, some of the conundrums of psychology, political science, ethics, and anthropology.

First, Then, to Psychology

Independence, autonomy, authenticity—whether in Freud's guarded aim of holding compulsion at bay, or in Jung's sunnier goal of individuation, or, finally, in the high noon of "I'm OK, you're OK," the solution to Humpty Dumpty's predicament is spontaneity. "Do what you want to do"; the trick is learning not to heed those voices, including inner ones, that would tell you to do something else.

Surely, then, the monastic life is the codification, the refinement, of everything the psychological revolution set out to overturn, for the monk is supposed to do what the superior says to do—the monk even takes a vow of obedience. Monastic profession appears to be the final, irrevocable rejection of the opportunity to become a fully realized human being.

If the life of a monk or sister were simply a tale of submissive compliance, the charge would stick. But the abbots and prioresses I know are quick to quash any illusions that their brothers and sisters are docile sons and daughters. My impression is that in the decades before the reforms prompted by Vatican II's decree on religious life, *Perfectae Caritatis*, the psychological binding of obedience was much tighter, more dangerous, occasionally lethal. I believe the current practice is much truer to the spirit of the Rule of Benedict, and here I believe the Rule is tied to the groundswell of human nature.

For the key notion is not obedience, but discipline. Discipline seems out of phase with spontaneity, but it is precisely here that monasticism has patiently nurtured an insight almost totally lost in our culture—namely, that discipline is the precondition for spontaneity. I say "almost," because there is enough vestigial awareness of the truth to have surfaced in a riveting *Newsweek* essay by Meg Greenfield in which she tries to account for Nelson Mandela's stunning impact on the city of Washington. "I decided his accomplishment was traceable to his much-vaunted discipline. This was his secret weapon—it is a very secret weapon in Washington, being the scarcest of all political characteristics. Mandela exudes it, and his story is a parable of discipline."[10]

Monks and sisters have been living parables of discipline, usually in less dramatic ways, for hundreds of years. While few monastics have been celebrities, monks and sisters nearly always impress those who get to know them with their remarkable individuality, their dogged resistance to fitting into the same mold. They have lots of options to choose from.

This insight into discipline and its intimate, essential relation to spontaneity is captured unforgettably in a single sentence at the end of the Prologue to the Rule, quoted earlier in chapter 5 about ecumenism: "But as we progress in this way of life and in faith, we shall run on the path of God's commandments, our hearts overflowing with the inexpressible delight of love" (Prol. 49). You would have to search long in the psychological literature to find a definition of spontaneity to match "inexpressible delight" for sheer pinpoint accuracy. This delight does not come easily. If you want to learn to pray spontaneously, you do not sit around waiting for prayer to come. You pray at 7:00 a.m. and noon and 7:00 p.m. whether you feel like it or not, and one day you may catch yourself praying at another time.

Here is what I see as the point of closest contact between Buddhist and Christian monasticism: the recognition that when we think we are acting freely we are almost always the victims of habits and compulsions that have us entirely in their control. Both the Buddhist and the Christian monk acknowledge the value of modern psychology's goal—spontaneity. The anomaly is this: the Buddhists have spent two and a half millennia, the Christians a millennium and a half, figuring out in a more clear-headed way than today's academic and medical gurus how to get there. The groundswell is still clanging the bell. People are listening. Thomas Merton's books are still selling well, and he has been joined in the ranks of bestsellerdom by the likes of Kathleen Norris and Joan Chittister, OSB.

Second, to Political Science

If monasticism serves psychology by putting spontaneity and discipline back together again, it serves political science by bridging the chasm between hierarchy and democracy.

Hierarchy is a term that deserves most of the bad press it gets these days, but almost everyone who detests hierarchy has to admit that the world cannot do without leadership. Not everything can be decided by everybody.

A superficial look suggests the monastery is a living fossil of divine right autocracy that has somehow survived the myriad forces of political evolution between antiquity and today. When the newly liberated peoples of Eastern Europe are looking to the United States as a form on which to shape their hopes (or at least they did in the immediate aftermath of the collapse of the Soviet Union), why would anyone be so foolish as to suggest that the United States look to the monastery for guidance and wisdom?

I make this suggestion because leadership in our society, in nearly every realm, has forgotten responsibility for discernment. Just as discipline is the substance for which obedience is the form, so discernment is the stuff of which the abbot's and prioress's authority is made.

The abbot or prioress is to pay attention to each monk's or sister's idiosyncrasies; everyone is to be listened to, especially the younger; all the monks and sisters are to honor one another. Somebody, finally, has to decide—there is no doubt who that is. But the test of the superior's success is not the decision. It's the quality of the listening that has preceded it. The Rule of Benedict trusts the intelligence and the wisdom of the people to a far greater degree than does the Constitution of the United States. The abbot or prioress is to listen, not because that is the way to disarm the opposition, but because paying attention to others is the way to hear God speak. Benedictine listening is very different from an opinion poll; it is almost its opposite.

Two political happenings in the year before I gave my American Benedictine Academy talk clanged the groundswell's bell for me with a clarity I had not known in a long time.

One was newly elected President Václav Havel's New Year's Day 1990 speech to the Czechoslovak people, a national leader's call to moral seriousness that resonates with the discipline of a Nelson Mandela. Listening to one another and even to oneself—Havel sounds like the Rule of Benedict—is essential. In Communist times, he said,

> We fell morally ill because we became used to saying something different from what we thought. We learned not to believe in anything, to ignore one another, to care only about ourselves. Concepts such as love, friendship, compassion, humility, or forgiveness lost their depth and dimension, and for many of us they represented only psychological peculiarities, or they resembled gone astray greetings from ancient times, a little ridiculous in the era of computers and spaceships. . . .
>
> We have to accept this legacy as a sin we committed against ourselves. . . . Freedom and democracy include participation and therefore responsibility from us all. If we realize this, then all the horrors that the new Czechoslovak democracy inherited will cease to appear so terrible. If we realize this, hope will return to our hearts.[11]

The other instructive political happening was the process by which Saint Benedict's Monastery (at the time still called Convent) elected its new prioress in 1989. It was not politics with a veneer of discernment. The election committee said that discernment "is indicative of slowness, gentleness, tentativeness, and collaboration, as opposed to speed and efficiency, absoluteness, competition, and control."[12] The process was so sacrosanct that up until the very last day the mandated response to the suggestion of a particular name as a candidate was a firm but gentle, "Sister, this is not a conversation I wish to have at this time." The process took many months.

It had been used in other monastic communities, but never before on the scale of Saint Benedict's. To make sure that every one of more than five hundred sisters was heard required a patience all but unimaginable in today's political and institutional life. I suspect there were sisters who thought the whole enterprise an unaffordable luxury and waste of time. It would have been easy, and entirely plausible, to say, "This plan is a nice ideal, but we have to be practical."

What the Sisters of Saint Benedict discovered is that the ideal was the most practical thing they ever did—they began the era of their new prioress with an understanding of their mission and goals that was truly their own. They had a prioress who had all the authority the Rule bestowed upon her, and she led a community that had been formed, and that had formed her, by the listening, the discernment that the Rule requires.

There is much talk these days, even in corporate America, about servant leadership. The monastery has known about such leadership for a very long time. To get beyond the impasse of hierarchy and democracy, the essential first step is to translate the whole debate into the terms of leadership and discernment.

Third, to Ethics

If monasticism's bell calls psychology to the marriage of discipline and spontaneity, and political science to that of leadership and discernment, it calls ethics to a fresh understanding of tribe and nation.

I use these terms in a quite general sense, to suggest the tension, evident everywhere in our world today, between the claims of the small group and those of larger entities. The global village turns out to be wracked by intense family feuds.

Through fifteen hundred years the Benedictine tradition has refined the Rule's insight that tribe versus nation is a category mistake for the reality of family and hospitality. Chapter 53, on "The Reception of Guests," comes fairly late in the Rule, after the family has been established and its routines detailed. It is precisely because the monks know who they are and where home is that they can freely welcome others.

Benedict's Rule is not one of the more humorous books in the Christian tradition, but I think we can all see him at least cracking a smile as he writes about guests, "monasteries are never without them." The phrase "never without them" is not just a description; it says something about the essence of the monastery. Precisely because the monastery is so unequivocally home for those who have committed themselves to live there until death, it is a haven for those who pass by and pass through.

I do not pretend to understand how this is so. As I noted in chapter 2, everyone I know who has spent time in the environs of Saint John's Abbey and Saint Benedict's Monastery attests to the uncommon, often unprecedented feeling of having been genuinely welcomed, yet the nature of Benedictine hospitality remains tantalizing, elusive.

The study of American society called *Habits of the Heart*, despite its flaws of scope and method, has highlighted the puzzle of identity and society.[13] The monastery proposes refashioning the discussion in terms of family and hospitality. There may be no more timely service monks and sisters could perform now for the sake of the world than to find ways to let the rest of us in on this secret.

Kathleen Norris, in the chapter of *Amazing Grace: A Vocabulary of Faith* called "Hospitality," puts this virtue in sharp contrast to "escape from the world" as exemplified by the Heaven's Gate group—who called themselves "monks" and died by mass suicide in 1997 in order to reach an extraterrestrial spacecraft. "Guests from the outside world," writes Norris, "are the one thing a cult such as Heaven's Gate cannot tolerate. Unlike the Benedictines, they really are trying to escape the world and can't afford to be contaminated by outsiders, those less enlightened than themselves, who are not true believers."[14]

There is an echo of this—faint, but unavoidable—in what Michael Medved wrote to Dreher, quoted in the introduction to Part Four: "When your child leaves home to go play with the neighborhood kids, you have to be able to trust that the values in your home are not undermined by the company he keeps." The monastery in the saltwater marsh, with its Benedictine options, is "never without guests." The Benedict option's ark, floating above the flood, has a door that opens only with a particular conservative Christian keycode.

Discipline and spontaneity, leadership and discernment, family and hospitality: monasticism's bell sounds new notes for psychology, political science, and ethics.

Fourth, to Anthropology

Anthropologists, accustomed to dividing things between sacred and secular, come to the monastery, hear about prayer and work, and easily fall into the trap of assigning prayer to the sacred and work to the secular, with an offhand tribute to monasticism for getting these two realms into some sort of balance. But this gets it all wrong, for prayer and work are not subsets of the categories "sacred" and "secular," but a whole different way of conceiving the relation between God and the world.

Years ago a monk friend said what I had long suspected but had never put into words: the chief characteristic of the monastic life is its ordinariness. Ordinariness is a word of revelation today, when spiritualities are proliferating, each intent on escalating beyond the others in the intensity of its claims and the extravagance of its terminology. In musical terms, Benedictine options are a rhythm of life that is *allegro ma non troppo*, more *legato* than *staccato*, and generally in the *mezzo-piano* to *mezzo-forte* range, with occasional moments of *pianissimo* and *fortissimo*.

Many current spiritual options insist on breaking down the sacred/secular distinction, but the very stridency of their insistence belies their fixation on the dichotomy. Meanwhile, monks and sisters go quietly about the business of living a coherent life as they have been practicing for about fifty generations, grounded in chapter 48 of the Rule, which is called "The Daily Manual Labor" and proceeds to talk about prayer and reading as well as what the title suggests.

The apparent distinction between *opus Dei* (the work of God: prayer) and *opera manuum* (works of the hands: labor), a distinction that signals "sacred versus secular" to the unwary and inattentive, is obliterated at the conclusion of the Rule (73.8): "Are you hastening toward your heavenly home? Then with Christ's help, keep this little rule that we have written for beginners." The *conversatio morum*, the "monastic manner of life" to which sisters and monks commit themselves, is of a piece; it is not sacred and secular spliced together.

Sometimes people who come to Saint John's and Saint Benedict's are disappointed. They are not sure what they expect to find, but they expect whatever it is will be unusually, maybe spectacularly, holy. They want to be dazzled by the sacred, overwhelmed by the *mysterium tremendum* (awe-inspiring mystery). What they find is people going about the business of daily life.

If they stay around long enough, these visitors may begin to realize that it is the very ordinariness of monastic life that is dazzling. The life of monks and sisters brushes away the modifier "merely" from the dismissive expression "merely ordinary," so that the ordinary becomes charged with the grandeur of God. As Emily Dickinson put it—she wasn't talking about a monastery, but she might have been—"I noticed, that the 'Supernatural,' was only the Natural, disclosed."[15]

The monk friend who alerted me to the ordinariness of monastic life also told me that even those who come not just to visit, but with the intention of joining the community, are often taken aback when they ask him to tell them about his religious experience, expecting him to mesmerize them with tales of heights scaled and depths plumbed, and they hear him instead say, simply and without elaboration, "I go to church."

I began ringing changes on the groundswell's bell by noting monasticism's staying power through history, and have continued through the sounds of discipline and spontaneity in the register of psychology, of discernment and leadership in political science, of family and hospitality in ethics, and of prayer and work in anthropology.

Fifth, to the Psalms

I conclude with what I believe is the peal of the bell generated by the deepest motion of the groundswell.

As I noted in chapter 5, I have come to realize that the psalms are key to the whole enterprise. It is they, ringing all sorts of changes on human nature and its relation to the divine, that remind the monk and sister every day, several times a day, that there is no simple, single mold into which a person of God fits.

In a single day the Benedictine rails against God, praises God, bargains with God, basks in the glories of nature, trembles before nature's terrors, thanks God for other people and asks God to destroy them all.

To switch metaphors momentarily from the bell to the organ, the Psalter is the diapason of the Rule and of the monastic life, for diapason is defined as the principal foundation stop in the organ extending through the complete range of the instrument.

To dig your spirituality out of the Psalter is to build a sturdy defense against any tendency to utopian illusion. People on the outside assume that Benedictines are striving to attain an ideal. Those on the inside are instantly suspicious of anyone who claims to know for sure what the ideal is. As I noted in chapter 2, Benedictines are constitutionally experimental. They will not let anybody turn them into an experiment.

Real community is a gift, not something constructed. This is a truth monastics know that the rest of the world needs to know. There is nearly everywhere today an intense, maybe even desperate, longing for real community. People are devising all sorts of schemes for "building community." But the monastery is a living witness to the truth that community is something that happens when the environment is right, when discipline and spontaneity, leadership and discernment, family and hospitality, prayer and work are rightly ordered—when *options* are functioning.

The Rule does not construct community, it hints at the necessary conditions. The groundswell's bell does not chart a course. It gives bearings from which to find a way—many ways, actually.

chapter eight

Learning from Father Godfrey and Sister Jeremy

I have stressed throughout this book that Benedictine options depend on evidence of the actual lives of real Benedictines. It is in their stories that the bell clangs in synchronization with the groundswell. As I noted at the very beginning, these lives show me a world in many colors—they extend my vision into the spiritual infrared and ultraviolet.

While there are as many hues as there are Benedictines, there is some merit, here at the end of the book, in focusing on two Benedictines it has been my privilege to know: Sister Jeremy Hall, OSB (1918–2008), of Saint Benedict's Monastery in Saint Joseph, Minnesota, and Father Godfrey Diekmann, OSB (1908–2002), of Saint John's Abbey in Collegeville, Minnesota. Their ways of being Benedictine are distinct, but they are linked through someone we met in chapter 5, Virgil Michel, OSB (1890–1938). Jeremy wrote a book about him. Godfrey worked closely with him and continued and expanded Dom Virgil's mission for decades.

In 2007 I had the honor, along with two of her sisters—Kathleen Kalinowski, OSB, and Stefanie Weisgram, OSB—of fashioning and editing from her lifetime of writings and retreat talks the Benedictine wisdom of Jeremy Hall, OSB. The resulting book is called *Silence, Solitude, Simplicity: A Hermit's Love Affair with a Noisy, Crowded, and Complicated World.*[1]

The title was not a slam dunk. About *Silence, Solitude, Simplicity: A Hermit's . . .* and *a Noisy, Crowded, and Complicated World,* there was no question. But what was to link them, fill in the elision dots? *Antidote to; Blessing for; Engagement with; Insight for; Prescription for; Love Affair with.*

We editors favored *Love Affair with.* *Engagement with* was the most serious alternative contender, but we argued that it didn't do justice to the book. "Engagement with the world," we said, implies a kind of distance—Sister Jeremy over against the world—tending even in the direction of Dreher's Benedict option. The book is about something much more intimate, passionate, involved. We took away from our reading of her text a deeper conviction than ever that the biblical story in general, and the incarnation in particular, are the record of God's love affair with the world—not God's "engagement with" the world. God "so loved the world" . . . not God "so engaged with the world."

As I noted in the introduction to Part Four, Dreher traces the coldness, deadness, and darkness of the world (as he sees it) to what he calls a fundamental "anthropological error." Right at the beginning of Sister Jeremy's book the contrast between the anthropology of the Benedict option and the anthropology of Benedictine options becomes sharp. The irony is exquisite. Sister Jeremy lived twenty-two years as a hermit (with her dog) in a trailer on the grounds of the monastery, which would seem to mean that she is Exhibit A for the Benedict option—flight from the world. That gets it backward.

Desire

The first chapter of *Silence, Solitude, Simplicity* is called "Desire: A homesickness at home." Hall notes that Pope Saint Gregory the Great, Benedict's first biographer, is called the "Doctor of Desire" by the great scholar Jean Leclercq, OSB, in chapter 2 of his book, *The Love of Learning and the Desire for God: A Study of Monastic Culture.*[2] The phrase "a homesickness at home" she takes from G. K. Chesterton, a hero of Rod Dreher's, but she ironically turns Chesterton's meaning inside out.

Chesterton writes: "The modern philosopher had told me again and again that I was in the right place, and I had still felt depressed even in acquiescence. But I had heard that I was in the WRONG place, and my soul sang for joy, like a bird in spring. The knowledge found out and illuminated forgotten chambers in the dark house of infancy. I knew now why grass had always seemed to me as queer as the green beard of a giant, and why I could feel homesick at home."[3]

For Chesterton, "the world" is the wrong place; feeling "at home" there is a mistake, an "anthropological error," so to speak. For Sister Jeremy, and Benedictine options, the point of monastic commitment—in her case, the hermit form of it—is to reestablish the world as home. The world outside the monastery is the right place—it's noisy, crowded, and complicated, not cold, dead, and dark. It's what Sister Jeremy was homesick for.

"The optimist's pleasure," Chesterton says, "was prosaic, for it dwelt on the naturalness of everything; the Christian pleasure was poetic, for it dwelt on the unnaturalness of everything in the light of the supernatural." I'm pretty sure Sister Jeremy would have countered with Emily Dickinson, whom I quoted in chapter 7: "I noticed, that the 'Supernatural,' was only the Natural, disclosed."[4]

Both Dreher and Hall highlight desire—the term appears 62 times in Dreher's 246 pages, 114 times in Hall's 170—but they interpret and evaluate it very differently.

Dreher has a thoroughly evangelical understanding of desire—our desires are basically corrupt, disordered. He believes modern culture is grounded in appeals to these base desires, and that "the triumph of the Self" has persuaded us that we can be truly ourselves only when we indulge them. The Christian is obligated to root them out.

Dreher quotes political philosopher Stephen L. Gardner: " 'It is in carnal desire that the modern individual believes he affirms his "individuality." The body must be the true "subject" of desire because the individual must be the author of his own desire.'"[5] Many references to desire in *The Benedict Option* are of this sort: carnal, own, individual, bodily, disordered; the "good of others" and "our own desires" are at odds; "for most Americans, desire is self-justifying"[6] (I suspect Dreher delights in the double meaning); one's own desires require "no" in order to say "yes" to God.

There are of course many references to the desire for God. Dreher is alert to the capacity of art to kindle desire. A huge fan of Dante, he notes that in the *Divine Comedy* "the pilgrim protagonist (also named Dante) learns that sin is disordered love. The source of all disorder is loving finite things more than the infinite God. Even loving good things, like family and country, can be a source of damnation if one loves them more than one loves God and seeks fulfillment in those things rather than in the Creator of those things."[7]

Here, as throughout *The Benedict Option*, there is no middle ground. If love is disordered, it's disordered all the way through. I'm not sure how to measure whether I'm loving some other good thing more than I love God, but I don't see as sharp a line as Dreher appears to draw. Most of the Benedictines I know don't see it either. In Benedict's vision "*the whole world* was gathered up before his eyes in what appeared to be a single ray of light."

Here is how Sister Jeremy's book begins. "We all need God. This is a fundamental human reality. We are radically incomplete and broken within; this is how we experience ourselves. Individuals who have sought a monastic life came to the monastery in desire, open to God's attraction, God's power to draw; but this openness to God's attraction is experienced by millions who know little or nothing of monasticism. Desire is the basis of community itself, as well as of each one's own response to God and to one another in community."[8]

"Incomplete and broken." At first glance, this sounds like Dreher. But notice how the condition is introduced. It's not because we are in rebellion against God, not because we have been seduced by a culture that has persuaded us that we are the measure of all things. No, it's "how we experience ourselves." The self (or Self) is not over against God. Love is not "disordered." It's blurred. Of the desire for God Sister Jeremy says this: "Like all good things, this desire can fade. Can we renew or reawaken it?"[9]

Yes, there are moments when *The Benedict Option* sounds almost like this, but Dreher's understanding of the dynamics of desire sets the passages in such a different context that they are actually dissonant, transposed into a minor key. For him, the good desire hasn't faded; it has been obliterated in "a world growing cold, dead, and dark." As I noted in chapter 6, Buddhists reflecting on the Rule illuminate Benedict's basically positive view of human nature—that, fundamentally, we are light and not darkness.

Mystery

If "desire" is one register of the distinction between the Benedict option and Benedictine options, "mystery" is another.

The term "mystery" appears only twice in *The Benedict Option*.

First is about the Middle Ages, when God's presence in sacred places, including those graced with relics, was acknowledged, but "the specific sense in which He was present was a mystery— and a source of speculation and contention even back then."[10]

The second is in a quotation of Supreme Court Associate Justice Anthony Kennedy's majority opinion in 1992's *Planned Parenthood vs. Casey*: " 'At the heart of liberty is the right to define one's own concept of existence, of meaning, of the universe, and of the mystery of human life.' " For Dreher, of course, this is an occasion for derision—one's "own concept" of "the mystery of human life" is "the end point of modernity."[11]

Missing from both of these is any glimmer of the rich, many-splendored portrayal of mystery in *Silence, Solitude, Simplicity*, where the term appears seventy-two times.

"We may try to reduce mystery to a problem," Sister Jeremy writes. "True mystery is a reality that is simply too deep for us to master. It is to be embraced and loved and searched ever deeper without ever exhausting it."[12]

> By mystery I do not mean the unintelligible or the essentially baffling, an enigma that challenges solution, or the darkness of the meaningless. By mystery I mean the inexhaustibly intelligible, the endlessly alluring, the depth of reality that invites us to enter again and again, to penetrate deeper and deeper, and that rewards us, not with a terminal or even a provisional "solution," but with nourishment for our minds, our hearts, our spirits. God is mystery; the human person is mystery; love, whether marital or parental, the love of friendship, or divine love is mystery; beauty is mystery; we ourselves are mystery to ourselves.[13]

She expands this into a meditation on the questions God asks us—"Where are you?" "What are you looking for?" "Who do you say that I am?" "Will you turn back and live?" "Where is your faith?" "Can you drink this cup?" "Do you love me?" Of the divine-human communication she says, "*there* is mystery" (italics hers), and goes on: "The divine questioning respects human dignity and human freedom. God's questions are caring, even when they constitute a reprimand or a challenge, and they are not merely rhetorical. As from a good teacher, the question is put in order to open up new dimensions of understanding or elicit new insights, correct faulty views or establish new links between things already known."[14]

This is radically different from Dreher's relegating mystery to either a source of contention in the Middle Ages or the end point of modernity. Mystery among Benedictine options is like a phrase of Matthew Arnold's: "not a having and a resting, but a growing and becoming."[15] Mystery entices, challenges, broadens. Mystery suffuses the monastery: "Benedict is careful not to stifle the spiritual liberty of each one by legislation that is too precise. And he leaves so much open to future interpretation and adaptation."[16]

Sister Jeremy got a hint of this when she was a child. "I am eight or nine years old. I am on the front lawn, lying in the thick grass under the oak trees. I am looking up into the expanse of a deep blue summer sky that seems to stretch silently, motionlessly, endlessly. I have an incommunicable sense of immensity around me, and aloneness in its midst. Not loneliness, not isolation—rather, it is a defining moment, a mysterious invitation into depths, beyond horizons I do not yet know."[17]

Sister Jeremy's many decades of Benedictine life, including her years as a hermit, were a coming to know those horizons she did not yet know—and discovering that there are ever more horizons beyond them.

Now, lest it appear that Sister Jeremy was beholden to always lofty theological terminology, it is instructive to hear how her colleagues remember her.

At her funeral, Prioress Nancy Bauer, OSB, said this: "Antonyms became synonyms in her life. . . . Mystic and mischief-maker. Witty and austere. . . . She believed in a practical Jesus and practical religion. She took her God straight up. No frills. No fluff. . . . I think what she would want me to say is this: prefer nothing whatever to Christ, but while you are longing to be with him in heaven, don't miss finding him on earth."[18] Another reminiscence is even more plainspoken: "Sister Jeremy didn't tolerate any bullshit when it came to God."[19]

From Caution to Boldness

"Damn! It is not the resurrection, but the incarnation." These words, reinforced with a hand pounding the desk, are vividly recalled when students and confreres reminisce about Father Godfrey Diekmann, OSB.[20]

He, like Sister Jeremy, believed in a practical Jesus and practical religion. For him, Christmas was theologically weightier than even Easter. He came near death many times. After one of these close calls, he wrote in his Christmas letter to family and friends: "Why the delay of sister death, of my final homecoming? Yes, it is time for repenting, especially for not heeding sufficiently Saint Leo's famous dictum [in a Christmas sermon], 'Christian, remember your dignity,' of sharing the divine nature, of truly being sons and daughters of God."[21]

Godfrey (born Leo) was the sixth of eight children of parents who had immigrated from Germany. Stearns County, Minnesota, was overwhelmingly Catholic. The role of the church was to sustain not only the faith but also German culture. The story of Godfrey the Benedictine, in his three-quarters of a century as a monk of Saint John's Abbey, is a tale of going, as Sister Jeremy did, "beyond horizons I do not yet know."

There were many horizons he needed to get beyond. During one of his sojourns in Europe he attended a performance of *Tannhäuser* in Paris. The next day he "saw a sign in the sacristy that put priests on notice: any priest, native or foreign, who attended the opera was suspended from offering Mass." The sign didn't stop him, but he celebrated Mass "with some hesitation."[22]

A much more ominous limited horizon was the suspicion of others, both Christian and non-Christian, imparted by the gauntlet thrown down by Pope Pius XI in *Mortalium Animos*, discussed in the introduction to Part Three: "this Apostolic See has never allowed its subjects to take part in the assemblies of non-Catholics."

As I noted further, there was planted early on in *Worship*, the journal that Godfrey edited for decades, an ecumenical seed that came to full flower in the aftermath of the Second Vatican Council. But Godfrey realized the flowering should have come sooner.

In responding to an award given to him in 1977 (the golden jubilee of both the journal itself and Godfrey's own profession as a Benedictine monk) by the North American Academy of Liturgy, Godfrey made a confession.

> As I look back, my single greatest regret is that, previous to Vatican II, *Worship* made almost no effort to become more ecumenical by enlisting, for instance, the help of Anglican, Orthodox or Protestant scholars in our common cause and concern. And this was definitely my own fault: for by this time my monastery had been pioneering in ecumenical work: the first ecumenical discussion between Protestant and Catholic theologians in America had taken place at Saint John's several years before the Council, and our seminary had been carrying on systematic dialogue with Luther Theological Seminary of Saint Paul. There is no excuse. I was shortsighted, not sufficiently catholic. Somehow, liturgy seemed too special, too sacrosanct, too uniquely Roman Catholic, to allow of accepting any advice from "outsiders." I have never publicly apologized for this. I now humbly do so.[23]

It was at the council that Godfrey decisively rejected both the suspicion in which he had been formed and the wariness his own monastery had already been pushing against.

Godfrey was a *peritus* at the council—that is, he was officially credentialed as an "expert" to help the council's commission on the liturgy in drafting and refining its documents. In those busy and heady days, Godfrey found himself most often gravitating "to the Protestant observers, who constituted, as one bishop confided to him, 'a group of dedicated men [sic] who have a grasp of the significance of this Council that should humble most of us bishops.' "[24] In the immediate aftermath of the council, when he was engaged in translations of the Mass into English, he urged his Catholic colleagues to plan "collaboration with Protestants."[25]

In a taped interview from 1987, Godfrey, reminiscing about a commission meeting in 1961 to prepare for the opening of the council the next year, formulates what I think is the essence of a central Benedictine option. He and some others were fervently arguing for authorizing the use of the vernacular in the liturgy. Cardinal Cigognani, president of the commission, objected. Latin was beautiful, traditional. No need for change.

Then a bishop from East Germany spoke, noting that life would be difficult for him if word of what he was saying got back to the authorities. He said that in a place where all external supports of the church were gone, Mass was all that the people had left. "They need to know what is happening." They need to recognize the words.

Godfrey said this is what the speech meant: it "gave us courage to be as radical as we possibly dared to be. It moved us from caution to boldness."[26]

That move—from caution to boldness—is something I've seen over and over again in Benedictines. It is very far removed from the defensiveness that motivates Dreher's Benedict option. Tradition is understood to be "*as* our ancestors did," not "*what* they did." Godfrey demonstrated his conviction about the inextricable linkage of worship and social justice when in March 1965, between the third and fourth sessions of the council, he participated in the civil rights march on Selma, Alabama. The sign he carried: "Selma is in Minnesota."[27]

Theology of the Heart; Stretch the Laws; Transfiguration

There are three features of Godfrey's story that undergird his quintessentially Benedictine boldness: his contagious theology of the heart; his regard for those who "stretch the laws insofar as required by the demands of life";[28] and attention to the transfiguration of Christ.

The very first verse of the Rule of Benedict admonishes the monk or sister to "listen with the ear of your heart" (Prol. 1.1). This conjunction of ear and heart is probably the single most referenced feature of the Rule in the plethora of current writings about monasticism and its relevance to our time. We mostly listen to pounce—that is, when hearing you, I am aggregating your weak points so I can squelch you. Listening is a strategy in a game of "Gotcha!"

Godfrey was widely credited with and admired for his "theology of the heart," which was grounded in "the conviction that the effort to grasp speculative theology would be successful to the extent that it was accomplished with reverence and awe."[29] One of Godfrey's favorite expressions summed this up—"You never know whether to do theology sitting down or to get on your knees."[30] The aphorism's "you never know" allows both head and heart to have a place—both/and rather than either/or.

The theology of the heart was not simply the substance of Godfrey's teaching. It was its effect—an infection. Theology "is contagious—or it ought to be," Godfrey said in a 1987 interview. His students remembered his pithy encapsulations of this contagious theology, such as "What good is it if the bread is changed and we are not?" and "All is gift." He once wrote to a friend who was apprehensive about teaching: "It is of course not unimportant that you present facts correctly; but it is even more important that your students are infected by your appreciation of these facts, and develop a similar love and gratitude and humility."[31] Love, gratitude, humility: a trifecta of Benedictine options, as both taught and lived.

In 1960, two years after Godfrey had first started working with what would soon be called the American Bishops' Committee on the Liturgy, he was informed by a colleague that the bishops "had not shown the least interest" in their opinions. Godfrey responded that nothing would happen "unless we speak out within the limits that the Episcopal Committee allows—but stretching those limits as far as possible."[32]

Just two years before, in 1958, Godfrey had introduced that colleague, Father Frederick R. McManus, to the readers of *Worship*. Many years later he praised McManus's "great ability to stretch the laws insofar as required by the demands of life."[33] McManus, though not a Benedictine, had a bungee-cord style that fit right in with Godfrey's tendency from caution to boldness. Benedict did, after all, leave open the option of doing something different from what he prescribed if it were better (18.22).

Incidentally, I know of no better illustration of this Benedictine inventiveness than what I reported in chapter 1, the response I got when I asked a monk what they do when a directive they don't like comes down from the bishop. "We post it on the bulletin board." Of all Benedictine options, this may be my favorite.

The corollary of Godfrey's grounding theology in the incarnation is his call to Christians in the Western traditions (those that for the most part have the Latin language in their past) to look East. He initially learned this in his graduate student days from Abbot Ildefons Herwegen, OSB, of Maria Laach Abbey, who said, "The whole of the Christian life can be summarized in the one word 'transfiguration.' Remember that." Herwegen went on to elaborate: "The difference between the East and the West is that the East speaks of light, and the West speaks of basic created reality. But light transfigures, like a piece of iron in the fire. So we are transfigured: we are in the light, we share the light, the life of God. That's what life means. And that's why life in the East has such a mystery. It is transfiguration."[34]

In Eastern Orthodoxy, Mount Tabor, the traditional location where Jesus "was transfigured before them, and his face shone like the sun, and his clothes became dazzling white" (Matt 17:2), is at least as significant as Mount Golgotha, the site of the crucifixion. The transfiguration, demonstrating that God's glory can shine in this world as it is, is understood not simply as a moment when Jesus's identity was confirmed, but also as a clue to what is possible for us—"sharing the divine nature," as Godfrey had learned from the Christmas sermon of Pope Saint Leo the Great, which was probably among the texts Benedict had in mind when he wrote in the Rule, "What book of the holy catholic Fathers does not resoundingly summon us along the true way to reach the Creator?" (73.4).

I cannot bid farewell to Godfrey without recounting the tale that for me—and many others, I suspect—most indelibly etches the portrait of Godfrey the monk.

Besides being a learned patristics scholar, Godfrey was also a mycologist and a cook, with a specialty of watercress soup. He regularly prowled the forests at Saint John's for mushrooms and watercress. In 1984 he "was looking for watercress and sank up to his hips in a swamp. Much to his embarrassment, he had to be pulled out by a truck hoist. His hip boots remain, to this day, at the bottom of the slough. He told the story in his Christmas letter with this addendum: 'What now bothers me is that during the entire ordeal of about twenty-five minutes I didn't have a single pious thought! What does that say of my more than fifty years of monastic life? Do I have to start all over again?' "[35]

What I so love about this is how, by the way he tells the story, Godfrey makes perfectly clear that it didn't bother him a bit. No need to start all over again. It was the more than fifty years of monastic life that prepared him *not* to have a single pious thought.

Connoisseurs of Surprise

Sister Jeremy and Father Godfrey, whose lives covered nearly the whole of the twentieth century and spilled over a little into the twenty-first, do not exhaust Benedictine options, though they exemplify a lot of them, and in different ways. Jeremy spent more than two decades as a hermit. Godfrey traveled the world many times.

Both of them were open, curious, and innovative, in the spirit of Saint John Henry Newman's "to live is to change, and to be perfect is to have changed often." Their truths were tethered to bungee cords, and they kept jumping until the end of their lives.

They were born into a defensive fortress Catholic world. They were prepared by their Benedictine formation to soar when the windows and doors opened—and they did their part in making the opening happen.

Godfrey and Jeremy were living examples of the "how" of the Benedictine charism that I outlined in chapter 2: experimental; rhythmical—devoted to the patterns of prayer and work; communal—yes, even Jeremy the hermit was acknowledged by her sisters as an integral part of the monastery; ecumenical; and narrational—they both knew how to tell the story of their own lives in the context of the narrative of their monasteries, of the church, of God's world.

Each of them demonstrates a way that Benedictines, even fifteen centuries into the story of their order, undergo the "enlargement of spirit" that Benedict himself reported.

Sister Jeremy's experience of "a mysterious invitation into depths, beyond horizons I do not yet know," is her way of seeing, progressively through her life, "all that lies beneath God."

Father Godfrey's "All is gift," combined with "love and gratitude and humility" as the goal of teaching, and transfiguration as summarizing "the whole of the Christian life," is also a way of discerning "all that lies beneath God." Benedict's vision—"the whole world was gathered up before his eyes in what appeared to be a single ray of light"—might well have been an echo of the biblical account of the transfiguration of Jesus. Godfrey "consistently proclaimed as his credo: 'I believe in one, holy, catholic, apostolic, and *changing* Church' "[36]—rebuilding, not restoration.

What, finally, is the consequence of implementing Benedictine options? It's the opposite of *The Benedict Option*'s withdrawal from "a world growing cold, dead, and dark." It's being alert to what God says in Isaiah (43:19): "I am about to do a new thing; now it springs forth, do you not perceive it?" The "new thing" appears in the world—the *whole* world—that Benedict saw in his vision. Benedictines are connoisseurs of surprise. Benedictine options aren't locked in a box. They keep popping out of it. Now and then they're even a wagonload of good trouble.

Before signing off, I want to address Benedictine monks and sisters directly: You have taught me much. I hope my holding a mirror up to you helps you see yourselves more clearly and inspires you to keep being yourselves, even to become more like yourselves. We need you to do this.

And now, to my non-monastic readers: Adopt or adapt at least some Benedictine options. You'll find yourself going be-yond horizons you do not yet know, taking your chances in the saltwater marsh, living the way W. H. Auden vividly portrays in "For the Time Being: A Christmas Oratorio," written in 1942, when the world was about as cold, dead, and dark as it has ever been: "You will see rare beasts, and have unique adventures."[37]

Notes

All references to the Rule of Benedict are to *RB 1980: The Rule of St. Benedict in Latin and English with Notes*, ed. Timothy Fry, OSB (Collegeville, MN: Liturgical Press, 1981).

Notes to Part One

1. Rod Dreher, *The Benedict Option: A Strategy for Christians in a Post-Christian Nation* (New York: Sentinel, 2017). Copyright © 2017 by Rod Dreher. Excerpts used by permission of Sentinel, an imprint of Penguin Publishing Group, a division of Penguin Random House LLC. All rights reserved.

2. Alasdair MacIntyre, *After Virtue: A Study in Moral Theory*, 2nd ed. (Notre Dame: University of Notre Dame Press, 1984), 263.

3. Dreher, 18.

4. Dreher, 236.

5. Cited in Patrick Henry, "A Minnesota Response," the final chapter of *Attitudes of Religions and Ideologies Toward the Outsider: The Other*, ed. Leonard Swidler and Paul Mojzes (Lewiston, NY: Edwin Mellen Press, 1990), 196.

6. Dreher, 99.

7. Dreher, 14.

8. *Second Dialogue*, 35, in Odo John Zimmerman, OSB, trans., *Saint Gregory the Great: Dialogues*, Fathers of the Church 39 (Washington, DC: Catholic University of America Press, 1959), 105.

9. Dreher, 242.

10. Jamaica Kincaid, "Mariah," *New Yorker* (June 26, 1989): 32.

11. Dreher, 76; repeated on 239.

12. Dreher, 40.

13. Dreher, 50.

14. Adolph Harnack, *History of Dogma*, trans. Neil Buchanan from third German edition, vol. 4 (Boston: Little, Brown, 1898), ch. 4, 311.

15. John Henry Newman, *An Essay on the Development of Christian Doctrine* (1845; 1878 edition; London: Longmans, Green, 1909), 1.1.7, 40; available also at http://www.newmanreader.org/works/development/.

Notes to Chapter 1

1. Babylonian Talmud, *Shabbat*, 31A, in Howard Clark Kee, *The Origins of Christianity: Sources and Documents* (Englewood Cliffs, NJ: Prentice-Hall, 1973), 160.

2. T. S. Eliot, "Little Gidding" (the fourth of "Four Quartets"; the poems known as such were published at different times and first gathered together under this title in 1943), sec. V, in *The Complete Poems and Plays 1909–1950* (New York: Harcourt Brace, 1952), 145. Excerpts by T. S. Eliot, copyright © 1936 by Houghton Mifflin Harcourt Publishing Company, 1964 by Thomas Stearns Eliot. Reprinted by permission of Houghton Mifflin Harcourt Publishing Company and by Faber and Faber Ltd. All rights reserved.

3. Adam Gopnik, "The Illiberal Imagination," *New Yorker* (March 20, 2017): 88.

4. G. K. Chesterton, "The Ethics of Elfland," ch. 4 of his *Orthodoxy* (1908) (London: John Lane, The Bodley Head, n.d.), 83.

5. Samuel Terrien, *The Elusive Presence: Toward a New Biblical Theology* (San Francisco: Harper & Row, 1978).

6. Dr. Seuss, *The 500 Hats of Bartholomew Cubbins* (New York: Random House, 1938), last page (no page numbering).

7. See "The Trellis," ch. 1 of *Benedict's Dharma: Buddhists Reflect on the Rule of Saint Benedict*, ed. Patrick Henry, with contributions from Norman Fischer, Joseph Goldstein, Judith Simmer-Brown, Yifa, and David Steindl-Rast, OSB; a new translation of the Rule by Abbot Patrick Barry, OSB; and an introduction to the Rule by Mary Margaret Funk, OSB (New York: Riverhead Books, 2001), 1.

8. "The Garden of Love," No. 44 of the "Songs of Experience," in David V. Erdman, ed., *The Complete Poetry and Prose of William Blake*, newly rev. ed. (Berkeley: University of California Press, 1982), 26.

9. Kathleen Norris, "The Rule of St. Benedict (A Sea Change)," *North Dakota Quarterly* 58/4 (Fall 1990): 166.

10. T. S. Eliot, "Choruses from 'The Rock,'" in *Complete Poems and Plays*, 106. Used by permission.

11. See Linda K. Fischer, *The Geography of Protestant Monasticism*, PhD dissertation, University of Minnesota, 1990, https://catalog.hathi trust.org/Record/102146053. Holy Wisdom Monastery, https://holy wisdommonastery.org/, near Madison, Wisconsin, a Benedictine women's community founded in the late nineteenth century, became in 2006—with canonical approval—the first ecumenical Benedictine community of sisters in the US. One of its members, Sister Lynne Smith, OSB, is a Presbyterian pastor.

12. C. S. Lewis, *Letters to an American Lady*, ed. Clyde S. Kilby (Grand Rapids, MI: Eerdmans, 1967), 2.

13. Quoted in David O'Reilly, "Chaplain Struggles with Catholic Stance on Female Priests," Knight Ridder News Service, published in *Amarillo Globe-News*, January 11, 2001.

14. E. L. Mascall, *Pi in the High* (London: The Faith Press, 1959), 7.

Notes to Chapter 2

1. Dreher, *Benedict Option*, 40.

2. MacIntyre, *After Virtue*, 263.

3. https://www.ilonasgarden.com/english-garden-style/, quoting Marina Schinz, *Visions of Paradise: Themes and Variations on the Garden* (1985).

4. Thomas Hobbes, *Leviathan* (1651) part 1, ch. 13: "Of the Natural Condition of Mankind as Concerning Their Felicity and Misery," https://www.gutenberg.org/files/3207/3207-h/3207-h.htm.

5. Theodore A. Gill Jr., "Canberra 1991: Stepping Stones and Stumbling Blocks on the Road to Unity," *Monday Morning* 56/7 (April 8, 1991): 16.

6. https://edsitement.neh.gov/media-resources/2019-jefferson -lecture-father-columba-stewart.

7. "A Conversation with 2019 Jefferson Lecturer Father Columba Stewart," Minnesota Humanities Center, October 3, 2019, https:// mnhum.org/blog/a-conversation-with-2019-jefferson-lecturer-father -columba-stewart/.

8. Imogene Blatz, OSB, and Alard Zimmer, OSB, *Threads from Our Tapestry: Benedictine Women in Central Minnesota* (St. Cloud,

MN: North Star Press, 1994). I had the honor of writing the foreword to this book.

Notes to Part Two

1. Dreher, *Benedict Option*, 1, 160, 82, 148, 202.
2. Dreher, 102–3.
3. Dreher, 148.
4. Dreher, 153.
5. Dreher, 241.
6. Jaroslav Pelikan, *The Emergence of the Catholic Tradition (100–600)*, vol. 1 of *The Christian Tradition* (Chicago: University of Chicago Press, 1971), 9.
7. *Babylonian Talmud*, Baba Metzia 59b: Tanur Shel Akhnai, at https://www.sefaria.org/sheets/144163?lang=bi.

Notes to Chapter 3

1. This chapter adapts material from Patrick Henry, "Monastic Mission: The Monastic Tradition as Source for Unity and Renewal Today," *The Ecumenical Review* 39, no. 3 (July 1987): 271–81. Used by permission.
2. Fyodor Dostoevsky, *Crime and Punishment*, trans. Richard Pevear and Larissa Volokhonsky (New York: Vintage Classics, 1993), 5.3, 405.
3. Fyodor Dostoevsky, *The Brothers Karamazov*, trans. Richard Pevear and Larissa Volokhonsky (New York: Vintage Classics, 1991), 2.5.4, 236–46.
4. Hobbes, *Leviathan*, part 1, ch. 13: "Of the Natural Condition of Mankind."
5. Dreher, *Benedict Option*, 97.
6. Cerinthus, in Irenaeus, *Against Heresies* 1.21, in J. Stevenson, ed., *A New Eusebius: Documents Illustrative of the History of the Church to A.D. 337* (London: SPCK, 1960), 95–96. I am well aware that there is an element of caricature in my treatment of Gnosticism. Discoveries in recent decades, memorably presented in Elaine Pagels's 1979 book, *The Gnostic Gospels*, and even more powerfully in her 2018 memoir, *Why Religion? A Personal Story*, make clear that the

term "Gnosticism" as used by early church writers blurs a wide range of nuances, some of which are at odds with my portrayal. I am using the term in Max Weber's sense of an "ideal type" in order to draw contrasts in fundamental attitudes as well as doctrines.

7. Marcion, in Irenaeus, *Against Heresies* 1.25.1, in *A New Eusebius*, 97.

8. *Against Heresies* 1.25.2, 102.

9. *Gospel of Thomas*, 56, trans. Stephen J. Patterson and James M. Robinson, at www.biblicalarchaeology.org/daily/biblical-topics/bible -versions-and-translations/the-gospel-of-thomas-114-sayings-of -jesus/.

10. John Dart, *The Laughing Savior: The Discovery and Significance of the Nag Hammadi Gnostic Library* (Harper & Row, 1976), ch. 16 ("The Laughing Jesus"), 107–13.

11. Pelagius, *In Defense of Free Will*, as reported by Augustine, *On the Grace of Christ*, 5, in J. Stevenson, ed., *Creeds, Councils and Controversies: Documents Illustrative of the History of the Church A.D. 337–461* (London: SPCK, 1966), 218.

12. Tertullian, *Apology* 50.13, in *The Fathers of the Church*, vol. 10 (Washington, DC: Catholic University of America Press, 1950), 125.

13. *Instructing the Unlearned* 25.48, quoted in Peter Brown, *Augustine of Hippo: A Biography* (Berkeley: University of California Press, 1969), 213. Brown's chapter 19, "Ubi Ecclesia?," from which this quotation is taken, is an excellent account of the ecclesiological issues raised by Donatism.

14. *Renew and Create*: 1969 statement of American Cassinese Congregation of Benedictines, http://amcass.org/documents/renew-and -create/. *Called to Life*: Statement of Federation of Saint Scholastica of Benedictine Sisters (requires password for online access). Joan Chittister, OSB, Stephanie Campbell, OSB, Mary Collins, OSB, Ernestine Johann, OSB, and Johnette Putnam, OSB, *Climb Along the Cutting Edge: An Analysis of Change in Religious Life* (New York: Paulist Press, 1979).

15. Gregory of Nazianzus, *Panegyric on St. Basil*, 63, in *A Select Library of Nicene and Post-Nicene Fathers of the Christian Church*, vol. 7 (New York: Christian Literature, 1894), 416.

16. Julian, *To Arsacius*, in Stevenson, *Creeds, Councils and Controversies*, 67.

17. Basil, *Longer Rules*, 7, in W. K. Lowther Clarke, *The Ascetic Works of Saint Basil* (London: SPCK, 1925), 163–64.

18. Martin Luther King Jr., "Letter from Birmingham Jail," April 16, 1963, in King, *Why We Can't Wait* (Mentor Books, 1964), 78.

19. "Letter from Birmingham Jail," 85.

20. "Letter from Birmingham Jail," 88.

21. "Letter from Birmingham Jail," 78–79.

22. "Letter from Birmingham Jail," 86.

23. "Letter from Birmingham Jail," 90.

24. "Repentance and Self-Limitation in the Life of Nations," in Alexander Solzhenitsyn, ed., *From Under the Rubble* (Bantam Books, 1976), 106–7.

25. "Repentance and Self-Limitation," 106–7.

26. "Letter from Birmingham Jail," 86.

27. Robert Bilheimer, *A Spirituality for the Long Haul: Biblical Risk and Moral Stand* (Philadelphia: Fortress Press, 1984).

28. Athanasius, *Life of Antony*, 5, in *Athanasius: Select Works and Letters*, in *A Select Library of Nicene and Post-Nicene Fathers of the Christian Church*, Series 2, vol. 4 (New York: Christian Literature, 1892), 197; available at http://www.ccel.org/ccel/schaff/npnf204.html.

29. *Confessions* 8.7.17.

Notes to Chapter 4

1. This chapter is much expanded from Patrick Henry, review of Chittister et al., *Climb Along the Cutting Edge*, in *Worship* 53, no. 2 (1979): 179–80.

2. Patrick Henry, *The Ironic Christian's Companion: Finding the Marks of God's Grace in the World* (New York: Riverhead Books, 1999), 92–96.

3. From an address by Mary Farrell Bednarowski, "Women's Creative Authority Will Save Religion, Theology, the Church (and the World): Sometimes It Helps to Take the Long View," delivered at Saint Benedict's Monastery, St. Joseph, MN, June 2, 2012, the 20th Anniversary of Studium, the monastery's research center. On that occasion I gave the response to her address.

4. Catherine Keller, "The Apophasis of Gender: A Fourfold Unsaying of Feminist Theology," *Journal of the American Academy of Religion* 76, no. 4 (December 2008): 906; cited by Bednarowski, "Women's Creative Authority."

5. Bednarowski, "Women's Creative Authority."

6. Jerome Oetgen, *An American Abbot: Boniface Wimmer, OSB, 1809–1887* (Washington, DC: Catholic University of America Press, 1997), 130.

7. Alexius Roetzer, OSB, to Boniface Wimmer, OSB, August 12, 1857, English translation in the archives of Saint John's Abbey, Collegeville, MN.

8. Promulgated by the Second Vatican Council on October 28, 1965; text in Austin Flannery, ed., *Vatican Council II: The Conciliar and Postconciliar Documents* (Collegeville, MN: Liturgical Press, 2014), 611–23; available also at http://www.vatican.va/archive/hist _councils/ii_vatican_council/documents/vat-ii_decree_19651028 _perfectae-caritatis_en.html.

9. Letter of July 25, 1859, quoted in Sister M. Incarnata Girgen, OSB, *Behind the Beginnings: Benedictine Women in America* (Saint Joseph, MN: Saint Benedict's Convent, 1981), 152.

10. Brian Patrick McGuire, *Friendship and Community: The Monastic Experience 350–1250*, Cistercian Studies series 95 (Collegeville, MN: Cistercian Publications, 1988), 415. Italics added.

11. Dreher, *Benedict Option*, 41–42.

12. Dreher, 75–76.

13. Dreher, 41.

14. Evin Rademacher, OSB, Emmanuel Renner, OSB, Olivia Forster, OSB, and Carol Berg, OSB, *With Hearts Expanded: Transformations in the Lives of Benedictine Women, St. Joseph, Minnesota, 1957 to 2000* (St. Cloud, MN: North Star Press, 2000), 37. Also available at https:// digitalcommons.csbsju.edu/saint_benedicts_monastery_books/5/.

15. Gregory the Great, *Second Dialogue*, 33, in Zimmerman, *Saint Gregory the Great: Dialogues*, 102–3.

Notes to Part Three

1. Dreher, *Benedict Option*, 136–37, 162.

2. Dreher, 136.

3. Dreher, 137.

4. *Mortalium Animos*, ch. 10; at http://w2.vatican.va/content/pius
-xi/en/encyclicals/documents/hf_p-xi_enc_19280106_mortalium
-animos.html.

5. September 11, 1987; text available at https://www.vatican.va
/content/john-paul-ii/en/speeches/1987/september/documents/hf
_jp-ii_spe_19870911_comunioni-cristiane.html.

6. Newman, *Essay on the Development of Christian Doctrine*, Introduction 21, 30.

7. Dreher, 10, 27, 87. For "Moralistic Therapeutic Deism (MTD)"
he references Christian Smith and Melinda Lundquist Denton, *Soul
Searching: The Religious and Spiritual Lives of American Teenagers*
(New York: Oxford University Press, 2005).

8. Jonathan Sacks, *The Dignity of Difference: How to Avoid the
Clash of Civilizations* (New York: Continuum, 2002), 66.

9. https://dimmid.org (click on "Introduction").

10. Kilian McDonnell, OSB, "Then It Is Finished, Done?," in *Swift,
Lord, You Are Not* (Collegeville, MN: Saint John's University Press,
2003), 26.

Notes to Chapter 5

1. This chapter adapts material from Patrick Henry, "Rule of
Benedict: Charter for Ecumenism," *Mid-Stream* 32/1 (January 1993):
59–69. Used by permission.

2. Martin Luther, "Eight Sermons at Wittenberg," no. 3 (March
11, 1522), in Theodore G. Tappert, ed., *Selected Writings of Martin
Luther* (Philadelphia: Fortress Press, 1967), vol. 2 (1520–1523), 244.

3. Geneva: World Council of Churches, 1982; also at https://www
.oikoumene.org/resources/documents/baptism-eucharist-and-ministry
-faith-and-order-paper-no-111-the-lima-text.

4. Joan D. Chittister, OSB, and Martin E. Marty, *Faith and Ferment: An Interdisciplinary Study of Christian Beliefs and Practices*, ed. Robert S. Bilheimer (Minneapolis: Augsburg; Collegeville, MN: Liturgical Press, 1983), 71.

5. Patrick Henry and Thomas F. Stransky, CSP, *God on Our Minds* (Philadelphia: Fortress Press; Collegeville, MN: Liturgical Press, 1982), 74.

6. *Orate Fratres* 12, no. 1 (November 1937): 1–2. Note: the journal was called *Orate Fratres* from its founding until 1950.

7. *Orate Fratres* 7, no. 9 (July 1933): 395.

8. *Worship* 26, no. 12 (November 1952): 570–71.

9. *Worship* 50, no. 6 (November 1976): 470–71. A similar note was sounded by R. Kevin Seasoltz, OSB, general editor, in 2001, in "Seventy-Fifth Anniversary of *Worship*: Our Editorial Policy Continues to Be Explicitly Ecumenical," *Worship* 75, no. 1 (January 2001): 4.

10. *Orate Fratres* 4, no. 1 (December 1929): 18–20.

11. The quotation is from sec. 5, par. 42, of the *1995 draft* of the Joint Declaration on Justification by Faith. The only text of that draft I have located on the Internet is in an Icelandic journal, *Gerðir kirkjuþings*, 1995, https://timarit.is/page/6491025#page/n113/mode/2up. The entire 1995 draft (in English) is at 101–18, the cited words themselves at 109. It's a pity that the rhetorical elixir of the paired "mutuallys" gets watered down in the approved 1999 text (5.40): "Therefore the Lutheran and the Catholic explications of justification are in their difference open to one another and do not destroy the consensus regarding the basic truths."

Notes to Chapter 6

1. This chapter adapts material from "Meeting, Practice, and Memory: What Monastic Interreligious Dialogue Contributes to Monastic Culture," *The Proceedings of the American Benedictine Academy Convention, August 12–15, 2004, St. Joseph, Minnesota* (New Series, vol. 8), ed. Renée Branigan, OSB (Dickinson, ND: King Speed Printing, 2004), 69–74. Used by permission.

2. This observation of Toynbee's is cited often, without specification. The closest I have come to finding an actual source is James L.

Fredericks, "No Easy Answers: The Necessary Challenge of Inter-religious Dialogue," *Commonweal* 137/1 (January 11, 2010): 10–13 (also at https://www.commonwealmagazine.org/no-easy-answers), in which Fredericks recounts a conversation at Sophia University in Tokyo with Heinrich Dumoulin, a Jesuit scholar of Buddhism, who related the remark made during Toynbee's visit to Sophia in the 1950s.

3. *Apologia pro vita sua*, ed. David J. DeLaura, Norton Critical Editions (New York: W. W. Norton, 1968), ch. 2, 79.

4. *An Essay on the Development of Christian Doctrine*, 1.1.7, 40.

5. Henry, ed., *Benedict's Dharma*.

6. McDonnell, "Then It Is Finished, Done?," 26.

7. From the transcript of the conversation, as also in subsequent references in this chapter.

8. https://www.la-croix.com/Religion/Approfondir/Documents/Le-testament-du-P.-Christian-de-Cherge-prieur-du-monastere-de-Tibhirine-_NG_-2010-09-03-578029; English translation at https://www.americamagazine.org/content/all-things/dom-christians-testament.

9. In Donald W. Mitchell and James A. Wiseman, OSB, eds., *The Gethsemani Encounter: A Dialogue on the Spiritual Life by Buddhist and Christian Monastics* (New York: Continuum, 1999), 262.

10. Thich Nhat Hanh, *Peace Is Every Step: The Path of Mindfulness in Everyday Life*, ed. Arnold Kotler (New York: Bantam Books, 1991), 26.

11. C. S. Lewis, *The Screwtape Letters* (New York: Macmillan, 1974), 16.

12. Dostoevsky, *Brothers Karamazov*, 1.3.11, 157.

13. Mitchell and Wiseman, *Gethsemani Encounter*, 266.

14. Jean Leclercq, OSB, *The Love of Learning and the Desire for God*, trans. Catharine Misrahi (New York: Fordham University Press, 1961), 44.

15. Henry, ed., *Benedict's Dharma*, 6.

16. McDonnell, *Swift, Lord, You Are Not*, 34–35.

Notes to Part Four

1. Dreher, *Benedict Option*, 90, 147.

2. Dreher, 40, 199.

3. Dreher, 203.

4. Dreher, 197.

5. "Views about same-sex marriage among Catholics," from the 2014 Religious Landscape Study conducted by Pew Research Center, at https://www.pewforum.org/religious-landscape-study/religious-tradition/catholic/views-about-same-sex-marriage/.

6. Dreher, 204.

7. Dreher, 200–201.

8. Dreher, 201.

9. Dreher, 200 (where dismissal of "preference" is couched in an endorsed quotation from Christopher C. Roberts, *Creation and Covenant: The Significance of Sexual Difference in the Moral Theology of Marriage* [New York: T&T Clark, 2007], 213), 43, 41.

10. Dreher, 197.

11. Dreher, 235.

12. Dreher, 75–76.

13. Dreher, 122.

14. Dreher, 99.

15. Richard Rohr, *The Universal Christ: How a Forgotten Reality Can Change Everything We See, Hope For, and Believe* (New York: Convergent Books, 2019).

16. Dreher, 93.

17. Dreher, 94, 56, 73.

18. Dreher, 180.

19. Dreher, 139.

20. Dreher, 155.

21. Dreher, 148.

22. See Patrick Henry, "The 'March for Our Lives' demonstration: Emma González's silence for the ages," (Minneapolis) *Star Tribune*, March 26, 2018, https://www.startribune.com/the-march-for-our-lives-demonstration-emma-gonzalez-s-silence-for-the-ages/4779 80623/; in print on March 27 as "4 Minutes of Silence Spoke Louder than Words."

23. Dreher, 161.

Notes to Chapter 7

1. This chapter adapts material from Patrick Henry, "The Ground Swell's Bell Over the Ebbing Sea's Roar: The Sound of Monasticism in Our Time," *The Proceedings of the American Benedictine Academy Convention, August 8–11, 1990, Yankton, South Dakota*, ed. Renée Branigan, OSB (Mott, ND: Eido Printing, 1991), 11–20. Used by permission.

2. Patrick G. Henry and Donald K. Swearer, *For the Sake of the World: The Spirit of Buddhist and Christian Monasticism* (Minneapolis: Fortress Press; Collegeville, MN: Liturgical Press, 1989). The book is dedicated to the monks of two Buddhist monasteries in Thailand, Wat Suanmokh in Chaiya and Wat Haripunjaya in Lamphun, and to the sisters of Saint Benedict's Convent (now Monastery) in Saint Joseph, MN, and the monks of Saint John's Abbey, Collegeville, MN.

3. G. M. Young, quoted in W. D. Handcock's introduction to G. M. Young, *Victorian Essays* (London: Oxford University Press, 1962), 10.

4. H. L. Mencken, "The Late Mr. Wells," ch. 2 in his *Prejudices*, First Series (New York: Alfred A. Knopf, 1919), 31. I have emended Mencken's "man" to "person."

5. Dreher, *Benedict Option*, 40.

6. Matthew Arnold, "Dover Beach," in *The Portable Matthew Arnold*, ed. Lionel Trilling (New York: Viking Press, 1949), 166–67.

7. Eliot, "The Waste Land," lines 22–24, in *Complete Poems and Plays*, 38. Used by permission.

8. Eliot, "The Dry Salvages," in *Complete Poems and Plays*, 131. Used by permission.

9. C. S. Lewis, *Surprised by Joy: The Shape of My Early Life* (London: Geoffrey Bles, 1955), 195.

10. Meg Greenfield, "Mandela's Discipline," *Newsweek* (July 9, 1990): 68.

11. http://chnm.gmu.edu/1989/archive/files/havel-speech-1-1-90_0c7cd97e58.pdf.

12. Rademacher, Renner, Forster, and Berg, *With Hearts Expanded*, 35.

13. Robert N. Bellah, Richard Madsen, William M. Sullivan, Ann Swidler, and Steven M. Tipton, *Habits of the Heart: Individualism and Commitment in American Life* (New York: Harper & Row, 1986).

14. Kathleen Norris, *Amazing Grace: A Vocabulary of Faith* (New York: Riverhead Books, 1998), 263.

15. Emily Dickinson, letter to Thomas Wentworth Higginson, February 1863, at http://archive.emilydickinson.org/correspondence/higginson/l280.html.

Notes to Chapter 8

1. Sister Jeremy Hall, OSB, *Silence, Solitude, Simplicity: A Hermit's Love Affair with a Noisy, Crowded, and Complicated World* (Collegeville, MN: Liturgical Press, 2007).

2. Leclercq, *Love of Learning and the Desire for God.*

3. Chesterton, *Orthodoxy*, ch. 5, at https://gkcdaily.blogspot.com/2017/07/the-flag-of-world.html.

4. Dickinson, letter to Thomas Wentworth Higginson, February 1863.

5. Dreher, *Benedict Option*, 43, citing Stephen L. Gardner, "The Eros and Ambitions of Psychological Man," in Philip Rieff, *The Triumph of the Therapeutic: Uses of Faith After Freud*, 40th anniversary ed. (Wilmington, DE: ISI Books, 2006), 244.

6. Dreher, 234.

7. Dreher, 226.

8. Hall, 3.

9. Hall, 3.

10. Dreher, 24.

11. Dreher, 44.

12. Hall, 124.

13. Hall, 84.

14. Hall, 124.

15. Matthew Arnold, "Culture and Anarchy" (1867–69), in *Matthew Arnold: Culture and Anarchy, and Other Writings*, ed. Stefan Collini (Cambridge: Cambridge University Press, 1993), 62.

16. Hall, 25.

17. Hall, 90.

18. Sister Nancy Bauer, OSB, "Funeral Homily for Sister Jeremy Hall," Sacred Heart Chapel, November 19, 2008. From the Archives of Saint Benedict's Monastery.

19. https://www.susansinkblog.com/2008/11/27/sister-jeremy-hall/.

20. Kilian McDonnell, OSB, "Godfrey Diekmann, O.S.B., 1908–2002, 'Teacher of the Century,'" in *Liturgy*, 17/4 (2002): 25; available at https://www.tandfonline.com/doi/abs/10.1080/04580630208599256.

21. Citation of Godfrey's letter, https://uscatholic.org/articles/201101 /a-vision-of-things-to-come/; Sermon of Leo (fifth century), https://www .newadvent.org/fathers/360321.htm.

22. Kathleen Hughes, RSCJ, *The Monk's Tale: A Biography of Godfrey Diekmann, OSB* (Collegeville, MN: Liturgical Press, 1991), 32–33.

23. *Worship* 51/4 (July 1977): 367–68.

24. Hughes, 227, citing letter from 1963.

25. Hughes, 266, citing letter of January 25, 1966.

26. Hughes, 191.

27. Hughes, 279.

28. Hughes, 118, re Fred McManus; also 178.

29. Hughes, 35.

30. Hughes, 52.

31. Hughes, 51, 91, 90.

32. Hughes, 178.

33. Hughes, 118, citing phone conversation, September 1989.

34. Hughes, 63–64, citing taped interview, November 1987.

35. Hughes, 312.

36. Hughes, 291. Italics in original.

37. W. H. Auden, *For the Time Being: A Christmas Oratorio*, ed. Alan Jacobs (Princeton: Princeton University Press, 2013), 65. Permission requested.

Note on the Cover

The cover is an illumination from *The Saint John's Bible* (https://saintjohnsbible.org/), at the conclusion of the Acts of the Apostles. It resonates with the vision of Saint Benedict—"the whole world was gathered up before his eyes in what appeared to be a single ray of light"—which figures prominently in this book.

The Saint John's Bible, commissioned by Saint John's Abbey and University, is itself a convergence of many Benedictine options.

A handwritten Bible may sound antiquarian, backward-looking, but the monks of Saint John's did *as* their ancestors did, not *what* they did. They recognized that after a hiatus of five hundred years, what is very old becomes very new once more. A Bible written and illuminated by hand, with persistence and patience over a period of thirteen years, is these days so startlingly countercultural that people all over the world—"to the ends of the earth"—take notice. Words, their flavor diluted in oceans of printer's ink, can suddenly be tasted again.

The Saint John's Bible reflects Benedictine commitment to ecumenism in the choice of the New Revised Standard Version of the biblical text. In its illuminations it demonstrates Benedictine openness to interreligious conversation by inclusion of the voice print of an American Indian chant, Muslim tradition from Ishmael, a menorah, Buddhist prayer wheels. Traditional fabric patterns from African textiles and a Peruvian feather dress surround the image of Adam and Eve. Native American basket weaving patterns surround the story of the loaves and fishes. Discoveries of science appear in strands of DNA and planets in orbit. Images from the Hubble Space Telescope reference the cosmic nature of the Word. Mathematical fractals dance around in the first strip of the "Creation" illumination. "The Fulfillment of Creation" features binary coding and mathematical equations in its background. Passages of the Bible that exhibit the role of women get special attention in the illuminations.

Donald Jackson, the renowned calligrapher who was artistic director of *The Saint John's Bible,* said that "the continuous process of remaining open and accepting of what may reveal itself through hand and heart on a crafted page is the closest I have ever come to God." Open and accepting, hand and heart, craft, revelation—these don't exhaust Benedictine options, but they are certainly part of the territory.

Also by Patrick Henry

New Directions in New Testament Study. Westminster Press, 1979; SCM Press, 1980.

God on Our Minds (coauthor with Thomas F. Stransky, CSP). Fortress Press and Liturgical Press, 1982.

Schools of Thought in the Christian Tradition (editor). Fortress Press, 1984.

For the Sake of the World: The Spirit of Buddhist and Christian Monasticism (coauthor with Donald Swearer). Fortress Press and Liturgical Press, 1989.

The Ironic Christian's Companion: Finding the Marks of God's Grace in the World. Riverhead Books, 1999.

Benedict's Dharma: Buddhists Reflect on the Rule of Saint Benedict (editor). Riverhead Books, 2001.

Orthodoxy and Western Culture: A Collection of Essays Honoring Jaroslav Pelikan on his Eightieth Birthday (coeditor with Valerie Hotchkiss). St. Vladimir's Seminary Press, 2005.

Flashes of Grace: 33 Encounters with God. Wm. B. Eerdmans Publishing Co., 2021.

Website: IronicChristian.org